HALF HOUR HERO

HALF HOUR HERO

Roz Purcell

PHOTOGRAPHY BY JOANNE MURPHY

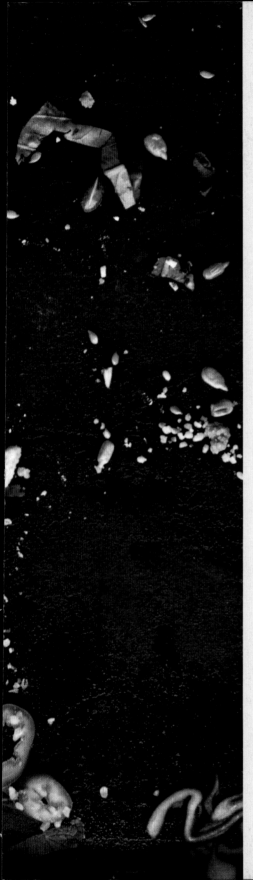

Contents

Introduction

People like to call healthy eating the latest lifestyle trend. So eating right and being active is a trendy new thing to do? Eh, I don't think so. We are all becoming more aware of the importance of looking after ourselves and the strong links between what we eat and our health. Back in my dieting days, my mum once pointed out that this is the same body you're going to have until you're a hundred years old (hopefully!), so if you're not treating it right now, how do you expect it to get you through till then? As we say in Tipperary, you can't put petrol in a diesel engine – you need to fuel yourself right.

About five years ago, I decided to do just that. I had been on a dieting rollercoaster ever since I started modelling at the age of 17. I've tried every fad diet out there, from cutting out entire food groups to living solely on shakes. My weight fluctuated for years, and it didn't help that I was working in an industry that repeatedly reminded me of that fact whenever I couldn't fit into my typical size 8.

But you don't have to be a model to relate to this. Even though I've left modelling behind, I still feel a lot of pressure from social media and I bet you do too. We're all trying to inspire each other, but it can also go the other way. Seeing a steady stream of beautifully tanned bodies with amazing abs on my Instagram feed can knock my confidence and make me feel like I need to look like that too, and fast, but now I stop myself from falling into that trap.

It's taken me a long time to get comfortable with my body and I only wish that I had known then what I know now about food and fitness. I learned a lot from modelling, not least the confidence to just be me. It forced me to take my health seriously by educating myself on eating well and training and it allowed me to discover my real passions in life: food and fitness. I also learned not to compete with others – instead, I use that energy to concentrate on myself and my personal goals. Dedicate your energy to being a better you, not some stranger you follow online. Be the best version of yourself that you can be in your own body shape.

> " DEDICATE YOUR ENERGY TO BEING A BETTER YOU, NOT SOME STRANGER YOU FOLLOW ONLINE. "

MAKING A CHANGE

I used to find myself mindlessly eating 'bad' foods, and sure, if I'd started, I might as well finish in style and get rid of all the 'bad' stuff in my presses, right? That kind of binge eating was hard on my body, but it was even harder on my mind. This, along with the 'no bullshit' school of parenting my mum and dad raised me with, spurred me to make a change.

So how did I do it? I started concentrating on all the foods I *could* eat rather than all the foods I couldn't have. I also tried to stop cutting foods out of my life, since it was having a negative impact on my social life as well. I couldn't even go out for a cup of coffee with a friend without worrying about the menu or feeling guilty. I stopped making excuses, stopped letting my body issues hold me back from doing things and started saying yes to life.

HALF HOUR HERO TO THE RESCUE!

So here we are. I started my *Natural Born Feeder* blog in 2013 to share my love of food and to spread the message of embracing a whole foods life. The blog led to my first cookbook, *Natural Born Feeder: Whole Foods, Whole Life,* which I refer to as the NBF encyclopedia. But even in the short amount of time since that book was published, my life has changed a lot. I've had the usual ups and downs and things have also become a whole lot busier, which means I've had to alter my lifestyle to make sure I can still prioritize the things that are important to me, which are eating right, training and surrounding myself with sound people.

It hasn't been easy. I realize now that I used to take time for granted. When I was modelling, I worked short hours and could leave my job at the door when I got home. Now that I work for myself, though, I have a lot less time for training and cooking. I went from doing two or three hours on the bike to train for a triathlon and spending hours in the kitchen to needing to do things fast. Let's just say that I can finally relate to anyone who has a hectic or high-pressure job and struggles to find the time to keep their diet on track.

> " THIS BOOK TICKS ALL THE BOXES: THE RECIPES ARE QUICK, HEALTHY, ACCESSIBLE AND FIT INTO A BUSY LIFESTYLE. "

Embracing this new on-the-go lifestyle was the catalyst for writing this book. I don't have lots of time any more for food prep or for training either, but I'm not willing to let them slide. We're all looking for a fast fix for everything – me included! – whether it's a HIIT session at the gym instead of a long run or a 30-minute meal instead of leisurely pottering in the kitchen for hours. That's where *Half Hour Hero* comes in, with over 100 recipes to help you leave your excuses at the door, get some meal prep done and get delicious, healthy food on the table in a hurry. This book ticks all the boxes: the recipes are quick, healthy, accessible and fit into a busy lifestyle.

I wanted to write a book that showcases fast, healthy dishes using basic ingredients that you probably already have in your presses, or if you don't, then at least now you'll know what to stock up on. All the recipes in this book take half an hour or less to cook, so whatever else might be holding you back, you won't be able to use a lack of time as an excuse any more!

> ❝
> I BELIEVE
> THAT FOOD
> SHOULD TASTE
> AS GOOD AS
> IT POSSIBLY
> CAN WITHOUT
> OVERLY
> COMPLICATING
> IT.
> ❞

REAL FOOD, REAL FAST

When I asked my readers what they wanted to see in my next book, one of the most frequent requests I got was for more everyday, easily accessible ingredients. I still love things like bee pollen or dried mulberries, but I know that I'm lucky enough to live in a city where I can easily pop out to any number of health food stores or delis that stock them and that those kinds of ingredients might not be widely available where you live. So through my blog and during my last book tour, I did lots of research on the staple ingredients that people commonly have in their kitchens and I've used these as the foundation for these recipes. I also realized that when it comes to a recipe for a quick, everyday meal, the last thing you want to see is an ingredients list as long as the page, so through a lot of trial and error I've created tasty meals that don't need a long shopping list. Besides, I believe that food should taste as good as it possibly can without overly complicating it.

Another excuse you often hear for people not eating healthy is that they think it's expensive, but I hope the recipes in this book knock that idea on its head. You should be able to pick up all the ingredients used in these recipes in your local shop and they won't break the bank.

FITNESS + FOOD

Fitness is a huge part of my life – if you follow me on Instagram, you'll already know that I'm at the gym almost every day. Food is my first passion, but fitness is a close second. Plus it goes hand in hand with healthy eating. When you train, you automatically tend to eat better. After putting in the time and effort, you obviously want to fuel your body right and not undo all the good work you just did.

But just like my time in the kitchen, I don't have a lot of time to spend on fitness any more, so my gym sessions are shorter and snappier. I've included a few of my favourite workout routines throughout the book to help inspire you, because dedicating even a little time towards keeping fit will reap big benefits. You don't have to spend hours in the gym – a 20-minute session is still worthwhile if that's all you can manage to squeeze in.

EXERCISE EQUIPMENT I USE AT HOME OR WHEN TRAVELLING

- Yoga mat for planks, side raises, stretching, leg raises
- Ab roller
- Chin-up bar over the kitchen door
- Skipping rope
- Boxing gloves and pads - perfect if you have a housemate
- Resistance bands

I also like to use timer apps, which are a great way to track your time spent working out. They help you to keep your breaks short and make sure you get that workout done with no procrastinating or time-wasting!

STRIKING A BALANCE

We should all make our physical and mental health a priority, no matter how busy our lives may be, but it can take a long time to achieve a balanced lifestyle. I hope these tips can help you to bypass some of the obstacles that I ran into and get you right on track. It's the small steps that you take over long periods of time that make the biggest difference.

- **FOLLOW THE 80/20 RULE**
My biggest piece of advice is to take an 80/20 approach to food. We're all human, so saying that you're going to be good 100% of the time just isn't realistic. You'll only be setting yourself up to fail and for a woeful amount of guilt to boot. This 80/20 approach is actually quite common. A lot of people live by it, proving its longevity as a lifestyle choice.

- **PLAN**
Plan, plan, plan! I talk about this more in the next chapter, but meal prep and planning is one of the biggest keys to my success.

- **EXPERIMENT**
There is no right or wrong diet and the best judge of what works for you is you. Certain foods may not agree with you, while other foods that different diets rule out might make you feel amazing. Don't cut out foods, much less entire food groups, before you've given them a chance.

- **EDUCATE YOURSELF**
Read the labels to figure out what's in your food and take back control. It's not up to anybody else to tell you what's in a food product and the manufacturer certainly isn't going to shout about it.

- **GET MOVING**
By now you know that I'm fanatical about training, but you don't have to be a fully fledged fitness jerk to move. Just move *more*: walk more, take the stairs more, join a gym. You'll enjoy it – and if you don't, then you probably just haven't found the right thing for you yet.

• WHAT'S YOUR EXCUSE?

If you feel like you're failing in your goal to lead a more balanced, healthy lifestyle, what's your excuse? Is it time? Money? Motivation? When you work out the reason, it will be a lot easier to find the solution. For me, in the beginning it was a lack of willpower. On the weekends I'd look at food as a reward and eat all the stuff I told myself I wasn't allowed during the week. Once I figured out that weekends are really no different to a weekday and I couldn't deal with the Monday guilt any more, I decided to have a treat if I really wanted one, no matter what day of the week it is.

• LET GO OF THE GUILT

I wasted so many years feeling guilty about food. I'd eat one thing I thought was 'bad' or not in keeping with my new diet and I would punish myself for being such a failure, either emotionally or physically in the gym. If you're going to have something a little naughty, just go ahead and have it, enjoy it and move on. Go back to your normal routine the next day and don't beat yourself up about it.

• THE DRIBBLE APPROACH

It takes time to adapt to new things, so make small changes. I like to call this the dribble approach. For example, swap your regular chocolate for dark chocolate, or if you've never cooked a meal from scratch before, start by picking one simple recipe a week to make, and in a month's time you'll have four new recipes in your repertoire. You don't have to dive in head first and try to do everything all at once. Rome wasn't built in a day and a balanced lifestyle won't be either.

> "
> YOU DON'T
> HAVE TO DIVE
> IN HEAD FIRST
> AND TRY TO DO
> EVERYTHING
> ALL AT ONCE.
> "

TIME TO GET COOKING

I didn't think it would be possible, but I'm actually more excited about this book than I was about my first one. Now that my lifestyle is more like my readers' and followers' long, busy days, I find that I'm getting a more enthusiastic response to the recipes I put on my website and I'm loving the new challenge of creating tasty recipes that take no time to whip up. I feel like this book really reflects me and my life now, and I hope that it will fit neatly into your life too.

1.

Meal prep

Meal prep is the real hero of this book. I usually train first thing in the morning and then run around town on photo shoots or interviews, but I still want to fuel my body right and I don't want to get depleted and run down. It's such a treat to be out on a job all day and know that I have a dinner waiting for me at home that will be ready in minutes.

Time management is another key to success. I've even had to alter how much time I give to training so that I have enough time for meal prep. It all comes down to good planning, whether that's sitting down for half an hour and planning out your meals for the entire week ahead or spending five minutes in the evening planning your meals for the next day. I'm obviously a big advocate of cooking for yourself, but sometimes you just have to eat out, so I'll even think ahead to where I can get a clean and wholesome meal.

Meal prep is also really helpful if you have a goal that you're working towards, diet-wise. When I've got a holiday coming up or I'm trying to get a little leaner, meal prep is absolutely key. If I really want to be the best, healthiest version of myself, I make a plan and stick to it. Plus when you know that your meal will be ready in half an hour or less, it saves you from mindlessly snacking and racking up lots of unnecessary calories.

Meal prep can be a hard habit to get into if you're not used to planning out your meals ahead of time, but when you commit to it and get used to the process, it becomes second nature. And once you see the benefits of planning and cooking this way, it will give you the motivation you need to stick with it. Meal prep cuts down on food waste, saves money and helps you achieve your goals – win-win!

This chapter includes my top tips for meal prep, my favourite meal prep utensils and my top 20 hero foods; a sample meal plan; and recipes for a few basic sauces and grains to cook in advance. Let's do this!

> "
> MEAL PREP
> IS REALLY
> HELPFUL IF
> YOU HAVE A
> GOAL THAT
> YOU'RE
> WORKING
> TOWARDS,
> DIET-WISE.
> "

TOP 10
MEAL PREP TIPS

1   On your chosen meal prep day, take 5 or 10 minutes to write down the recipes you want to make or prep in advance, then make your shopping list accordingly.

2   Plan different meals, but try to pick ones with similar ingredients so that your shopping list isn't overwhelming. For example, the same basic ingredients can be used various ways, like the two egg muffins on pages 62–63 and the two chicken tray bakes on pages 154 and 158.

3   You don't have to do all your prep in one day. Sometimes I see people online showing off a whole week's worth of cooking done on a Sunday, but that doesn't mean you have to do it that way. You can break it up throughout the week or even do your prep on Saturday and cook on Sunday to spread out the workload.

4   When you do your meal prep, you don't necessarily have to do all of it. Sometimes the majority of my prep simply involves having all my veg peeled, sliced or spiralized and my ingredients all portioned up and ready to go in ziplock bags or airtight containers.

5 Avocados deserve their very own point here! It's frustrating when you can't find a ripe avocado, or even worse, when you do have one but you let it get overripe. I get around this problem by blending my perfectly ripe avocados with some lime or lemon juice and spooning the purée into an ice cube tray to freeze, then popping out the cubes and storing them in a ziplock bag in the freezer to have on hand for smoothies. I do the same thing with any fruit that's about to go off if I won't get to use it in time, which is also perfect for adding to smoothies or porridge.

6 Cook a double batch. Some weeks I'm so busy that I don't have time to prep at all, but I stay on track by cooking a double batch every time I make dinner or lunch, which means I'll still be sorted for the next day. For example, I try to cook double on a Sunday so that Monday's dinner is sorted, then on Monday I'll cook ahead for Tuesday or Wednesday. A lot of recipes in this book don't even take a full half hour to make, so you could even make a few at a time in advance.

7 Invest in good food prep utensils (check out my list on the next page) and a slow cooker too. Slow cookers are so handy for meal prep, but I'm afraid you won't find any slow cooker recipes in this book because they don't fit in with the half-hour timeframe. I have loads of recipes on my website, though, so check them out at www.naturalbornfeeder.com.

8 It's time to form a deeper relationship with your freezer. Clean it out and make good use of it. If you're making double batches, freeze the extra half for later in the week.

9 Portion out immediately, especially when prepping snacks. Sometimes you can eat half the batch just while you're making it – I'm speaking from experience here! – so have your jars or ziplock bags ready.

10 Prep like a pro! I like to set up mini stations to make my work more organized. I usually set up four stations: clean and wash; peel and slice; cook; and assemble and pack.

TOP 10
MEAL PREP UTENSILS

1. **AIRTIGHT CONTAINERS:**
Invest in good-quality airtight containers – and don't let anyone borrow them!

2. **CHOPPING BOARD SET:**
A must for meal prep stations. I like to use the colour-coded ones for meat, fish, veg and raw food.

3. **GOOD KNIVES:**
If you take cooking at all seriously, then you'll respect and value a good knife.

4. **JARS:**
I store all kinds of things in jars, such as sauces, dressings, protein balls, nut and seed mixes and homemade nut butters. There's no need to buy new ones – save the jars from shop-bought jams or sauces, give them a good wash and reuse them for storage.

5. **JULIENNE PEELER:**
This is a quicker and cheaper way to get the same effect as a spiralizer.

6. **MANDOLIN SLICER:**
This may be the most dangerous piece of kitchen equipment I own – watch your fingers and always use the guard, because that blade is super sharp – but it makes short work of slicing veggies.

7. **MEASURING SPOONS AND KITCHEN SCALE:**
A set of measuring spoons and a kitchen scale are both a must, particularly for baking. Let's not have any guesstimation here – use the exact measurements provided in the recipe. It's a no-fail no-brainer!

8. **MUFFIN TRAYS:**
Aside from the obvious things like muffins and chocolate cups, muffin trays are great for savoury recipes too and for making things into individual portions, like egg muffins and mini meatloaves, or modifying a bread recipe into buns.

9. **NUTRIBULLET:**
For smoothies, sauces, protein balls, batters, pancakes, soups and more, it's the perfect little sous chef!

10. **ZIPLOCK BAGS:**
I use these a lot for portioning and storing my prepped ingredients as well as for storing bars and snacks in the fridge without taking up too much space.

MY TOP 20
HERO FOODS

- Almond milk
  (unsweetened)
- Avocados
- Bananas
- Berries
- Broccoli
- Chia seeds
- Courgettes
- Dark chocolate
- Eggs
- Feta
- Lemons
- Maple syrup and honey
- Nut butter
- Porridge oats
- Protein powder
- Raw nuts and seeds
- Rice, lentils and
  quinoa
- Sweet potatoes
- Tinned tomatoes,
  chickpeas and beans
- Yogurt

SAMPLE MEAL PLAN

Let me give you an example of how I plan out my meals. I pick two breakfast meals (one sweet and one savoury), two lunch options, two dinner options and two snacks that I can make ahead or in bulk and I vary them throughout the week. I try to choose recipes that use similar ingredients but have different tastes so that I don't get bored. It also helps to streamline your shopping.

Here's a sample meal plan (which also just so happens to be vegan):

BREAKFAST:
- Sweet potato waffles with quick beans
- Blueberry breakfast bars

LUNCH:
- Cashew, bean and oat burger
- Spicy bean and bulgur soup

DINNER:
- Peanut, squash and chickpea curry
- The tastiest veggie stew

SNACKS:
- Snappy seeds
- Peanut butter and raspberry oat scones

> "
> MEAL PREP CUTS DOWN ON FOOD WASTE, SAVES MONEY AND HELPS YOU ACHIEVE YOUR GOALS - WIN-WIN!
> "

STAPLES TO MAKE AHEAD

Basil pesto

MAKES 1 SMALL JAR

85g fresh basil leaves
50g cashews
2 garlic cloves, peeled
2 tbsp olive oil
2 tbsp grated Parmesan cheese
(or nutritional yeast for a vegan
option)

Put the basil, cashews and garlic in a pestle and mortar and pound into a paste, but with some bits of cashew still visible. Stir in the olive oil and nutritional yeast or Parmesan, then spoon the pesto into a clean jar. If you'll be storing this in the fridge (it will keep for up to a week), pour another tablespoon of olive oil on top to prevent the pesto from turning brown.

Red pesto

MAKES 1 SMALL JAR

1 x 260g jar or 20 sun-dried
tomatoes in olive oil, drained
80g Brazil nuts or almonds
2 garlic cloves, peeled
4 tbsp olive oil
3 tbsp grated Parmesan cheese
(or nutritional yeast for a vegan
option)

Pop the sun-dried tomatoes into a food processor and blend into a smooth paste. Put the nuts and garlic in a pestle and mortar and pound until they've been crushed into tiny pieces, then stir in the sun-dried tomato purée, olive oil and nutritional yeast or Parmesan. Spoon the pesto into a clean jar. If you'll be storing this in the fridge (it will keep for up to a week), pour another tablespoon of olive oil on top to prevent the pesto from turning brown.

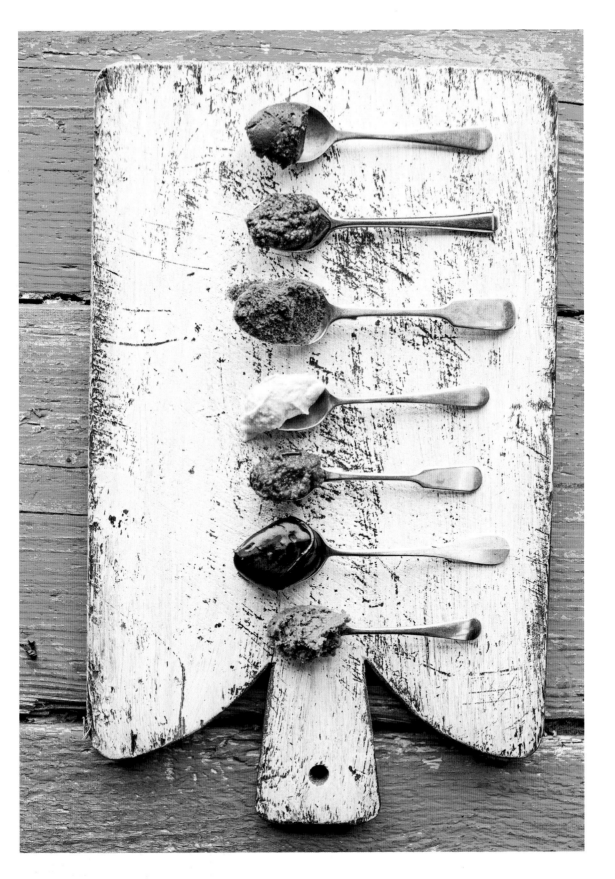

Hummus

MAKES 250G

1 x 400g tin of chickpeas, drained
    and rinsed
juice of 1 lemon
4 tbsp olive oil
2 tbsp tahini
2 tsp ground cumin
1 tsp paprika

Put all the ingredients in a
blender and blitz until smooth.
You can store this hummus
in an airtight container in the
fridge for up to six days. For
a few variations on this basic
version, try adding one roasted
red pepper, 4 tablespoons of
chopped fresh coriander or
one cooked beetroot.

Green mayo

MAKES 1 SMALL JAR

If you're using egg whites in
the porridge recipes in this
book, this is a great way to
use up the leftover yolks –
plus it's amazing with sweet
potato fries!

2 egg yolks
2 tbsp chopped fresh basil
2 tsp apple cider vinegar
1 tsp Dijon mustard
5 tbsp olive oil

Put the egg yolks, basil,
vinegar and mustard in a
large bowl and whisk them
together until well combined
(an electric whisk works well
for this). Slowly add the oil a
little at a time while whisking
continuously. It should start to
get thick. Keep adding the oil,
bit by bit, until you reach your
desired consistency. Spoon
into a clean glass jar and store
in the fridge for up to five days.

Curry spice mix

MAKES 4½ TEASPOONS

2 tsp ground coriander
1 tsp ground cumin
½ tsp ground turmeric
½ tsp chilli powder or cayenne
    pepper
½ tsp ground cinnamon

Mix all the spices together in a
small bowl, then store in a small
jar in a cool, dry place for up to
six months.

Notella

MAKES 1 SMALL JAR

100g raw or roasted hazelnuts
2 tbsp coconut oil
4 tbsp raw cacao powder
4 tbsp unsweetened hazelnut or
    almond milk
4 tbsp maple syrup
1 tsp vanilla extract
pinch of sea salt

If using raw hazelnuts, you can keep the skins on them. If you're roasting the nuts yourself, rub off the skins in a clean tea towel for a smoother spread. Start by melting the coconut oil in a small pan set over a low heat. Put all the ingredients, including the melted coconut oil, in a food processor or blender (a NutriBullet works well) and blend into a smooth, creamy spread. Spoon into a clean jar and store in the fridge for up to 10 days.

Chocolate sauce

MAKES 1 SERVING

2 tbsp maple syrup or honey
1 tbsp raw cacao powder

To make the sauce, just whisk the maple syrup and cacao powder together in a cup.

Curry paste

MAKES 1 SMALL JAR

4 garlic cloves, peeled and chopped
5cm piece of fresh ginger, peeled
    and chopped
4 large red or green fresh chillies,
    deseeded and chopped
zest and juice of 1 lime
2 tbsp chopped fresh coriander
    leaves
2 tbsp tomato purée
1 tbsp ground cumin
1 tbsp ground coriander
1 tsp ground turmeric
1 tsp ground black pepper
1 tsp lemongrass paste (*optional*)

Put all the ingredients in a food processor and blend into a smooth paste. Store in a glass jar in the fridge for up to a week.

HOW TO PREP
SOME BASICS

Cooking a big batch of grains or prepping vegetables like cauli rice or spiralized courgettes on a Sunday and having them on hand in the fridge for the days ahead means you can get many of the recipes in this book on the table in half an hour from start to finish. I've used cup measurements in these recipes because they're the easiest way of learning the ratio of grain to liquid, such as one part quinoa to two parts water. The yields are based on an American-style cup measurement, but the main thing is to keep the ratio right.

Bulgur wheat

I love bulgur wheat for lots of reasons, but the main one is because it's so easy to prep. Put some bulgur in a heatproof bowl and pour in just enough boiling water to cover. Give it a quick stir and cover the bowl with a lid or plate or a piece of clingfilm – you need something to lock in the heat. Leave for 20 minutes, then remove the lid and fluff up the bulgur with a fork. The water should be fully absorbed, so you shouldn't need to drain it. If you're making this ahead of time, let the bulgur cool completely before storing it in an airtight container in the fridge for up to five days.

Curvy courgetti
MAKES 1 SERVING

Wash a good-sized courgette and cut off the top and bottom (I like to keep courgettes unpeeled for this), then make 'noodles' by using a julienne peeler or spiralizer. Store in an airtight container or ziplock bag for up to three days in the fridge or you could even stash these in the freezer. To cook, you can steam the noodles for 2 minutes, until lightly wilted, or flash-fry in a hot pan with a little olive oil, but I also love spiralized courgette raw with a dollop of pesto (page 32) and some toasted seeds.

> ❝
> MEAL PREP MEANS YOU CAN GET MANY OF
> THE RECIPES IN THIS BOOK ON THE TABLE
> IN HALF AN HOUR FROM START TO FINISH.
> ❞

Perfect perky rice

MAKES 600G COOKED RICE

Put 1 cup of rice (175g to 200g of rice, depending on whether it's brown or white rice) in a sieve and rinse it under cold running water until the water runs clear (this helps make the rice nice and fluffy when it's done, so don't be tempted to skip this step). Transfer to a medium-sized saucepan and add 1½ cups of water and a pinch of salt. Cover the pot and bring to the boil, then turn the heat down and simmer for about 20 minutes, until all the water has been absorbed and the rice is tender. Don't lift the lid to peek into the pan or you'll release all the heat. When the 20 minutes are up, remove from the heat, take the lid off and put a clean tea towel on top of the pan, then put the lid back on and let it sit for 15 minutes. Fluff up the rice with a fork before serving. Don't use a spoon or it will clump together and undo all your hard work to get it fluffy.

If you want to cook rice ahead of time, it's very important that you don't let it sit around at room temperature for more than an hour, otherwise you run the risk of getting food poisoning and no one wants that! Cool it down as quickly as possible, store it in an airtight container in the fridge for only up to one day, reheat it until it's steaming hot all the way through and never reheat cooked rice more than once.

Cauliflower rice

SERVES 2

Cauliflower rice is a great way of keeping your carbohydrates low. It's so easy to make: remove the leaves and stem and cut the cauliflower into large pieces, trimming out the inner core. Put in a food processor and pulse until the cauliflower is the texture of couscous. *Et voilà* – cauliflower rice! It needs some help in the taste department, but don't worry, I've got you covered with the recipes in this book. You can store the uncooked cauliflower rice in an airtight container in the fridge for up to three days or freeze it.

Split red lentils

MAKES 500G COOKED LENTILS

I like red lentils best because the texture is softer and because they cook the fastest. Put 1 cup of dried lentils in a sieve and give them a good rinse. Transfer to a medium-sized saucepan and pour in 1½ cups of water, broth or stock. Bring to the boil, reduce the heat and simmer for 10 to 15 minutes, stirring now and then. Don't cook them for longer or they'll get mushy. If making ahead of time, let the lentils cool completely before storing in an airtight container in the fridge for up to five days.

Fluffy quinoa

MAKES 550G COOKED QUINOA

Put 1 cup of quinoa in a sieve and rinse it to get rid of its bitter coating. Transfer to a medium-sized saucepan and pour in 2 cups of water. Cover and bring to the boil, then turn the heat down to low and cook, still covered, for 15 minutes. Remove from the heat and let it stand for 5 minutes with the lid on – no peeking! Fluff up with a fork before serving. If making ahead of time, let the quinoa cool completely before storing in an airtight container in the fridge for up to five days.

2.

Smoothies + tonics

SMOOTHIES

I like my smoothies to be thick and creamy, so my liquid measurements are on the low side. If you like yours a little thinner, just add some extra liquid. You can also replace bananas with avocados and dates with honey or maple syrup in all these recipes. I always peel and dice a few soft bananas and store them in ziplock bags in the freezer to add instant creaminess and freshness to my smoothies. I also love to add supplements to my smoothies, which you might want to try too if you think it would complement your diet.

THINGS I LIKE TO ADD TO
MY SMOOTHIES:

- Spirulina
- Flax oil
- Probiotics
- Maca powder
- L-glutamine powder
- Vanilla powder
- Protein - I love a pea/rice/hemp protein mix
  or a good-quality whey protein powder
- Spices, such as cinnamon, turmeric and
  cardamom
- Fresh herbs, such as parsley, basil and mint
- Oats for a post-workout smoothie
- Hemp seeds or cacao nibs to garnish for a
  little added crunch
- Raw honey

Put all the ingredients in a blender or food processor and blitz until smooth. Pour into a tall glass and drink up or pour the smoothie into a jar and stash it in your gym bag to have later.

#wokeuplikethis

Coffee is my little pre-workout wake-me-up, but unlike most people, I don't love it all on its lonesome, so I need to boost mine up and turn it into a creamy, kick-ass drink.

300ml almond milk
1–2 shots of espresso
1 banana, peeled, sliced and frozen
1 tbsp almond or cashew butter

Berry awake!

A simple mash-up of all the things you need to give you that wide-awake feeling!

250ml coconut water
juice of ½ lemon
2 handfuls of frozen berries
handful of raw walnuts
1 tbsp goji berries, soaked, or 1 tsp honey (*optional for added sweetness*)
1 tbsp flaxseeds or chia seeds
pinch of ground cinnamon

Spice it up

My new favourite smoothie! I love this for breakfast on the run or as a little pick-me-up an hour before a gym session. Don't fear the little kick of heat, I swear it's super nice.

350ml almond milk
1 scoop of your favourite vanilla protein powder (I use a pea hemp mix)
1 Medjool date, pitted (*optional for extra sweetness if your protein is unsweetened*)
1 tbsp vanilla powder
1 tbsp maca powder
1 tbsp almond butter
1½ tsp ground cinnamon
¼ tsp cayenne pepper
pinch of sea salt

Da real MVP

A seemingly simple smoothie, but it's packed full of greens to ramp up those Popeye vibes!

400ml coconut water
½ ripe avocado, peeled, stoned, diced and frozen
1 small kiwi, peeled
½ cucumber, diced
handful of baby spinach or kale
2.5cm piece of fresh ginger, peeled and chopped
2 fresh mint leaves
2 tbsp fresh flat-leaf parsley leaves
handful of ice

The break-up shake-up

When all you crave is something indulgent and comforting but you still want to look your best, this smoothie is your new soulmate.

250ml almond milk
1 large banana, peeled, sliced and frozen
1–2 Medjool dates (because I had none, get it?), pitted
1 tbsp raw cacao powder
1 tbsp cacao nibs
1 tbsp peanut butter
handful of ice
cacao nibs, to garnish

Orange you glad

I love adding cardamom to this smoothie sometimes. It's also a great post-workout option if you add a banana. (As for the name, let's just say it's a personal joke that involves a dodgy tan . . .)

250ml freshly squeezed orange juice (about 2 oranges)
½ ripe avocado, peeled and stoned
6 green grapes
2 handfuls of baby spinach
3 fresh mint leaves
2 fresh basil leaves
pinch of ground cardamom (*optional*)
handful of ice

THE BREAK-UP
SHAKE-UP

Phuk it, drink up!

This is the smoothie I would get when I was on holiday in Phuket (hence the name). It's a tropical drink to make you feel like you're back on your favourite beach and not staring out at the cold rain.

250ml coconut milk

juice of ½ lime

½ ripe mango, peeled and diced

2 tbsp coconut meat

handful of ice

The pre-game

Get your game face on – it's time to hit the gym and power through your killer session!

300ml coconut water

handful of frozen blueberries or strawberries

3 fresh pineapple chunks

1 scoop of vanilla protein powder

1 shot of beet juice or ½ small beet, scrubbed and grated

pinch of ginseng powder (*optional*)

handful of ice (*optional*)

MY FAVOURITE BIKE BLITZ

Warm up on the bike for 3 minutes, moving through the gears.

- Do 20 seconds at your max speed then 10 seconds of low intensity x 8 rounds + a 1-minute recovery break, spinning out your legs. Repeat this entire sequence four times.

- Cool down by spinning out your legs and make sure to stretch afterwards. For the final set I push up the resistance to give it the last bit I have left in me.

THE PRE-GAME

The 'BRB' chocolate milk

Chocolate milk always reminds me of my sister's boyfriend after a GAA match, but this version is good for an everyday gal, served up hot or cold. For extra creaminess if you're making it hot, add a tablespoon of cashew butter and blend until frothy.

250ml almond milk

2 Medjool dates, pitted

1 tbsp raw cacao powder

1 tbsp cashew butter (*optional – see note*)

1 tsp vanilla powder or extract

pinch of sea salt

Post-workout powerhouse

It's important to recover right after a proper session to rebuild and restore those working muscles, so drink up and feel smug! Don't forget to get some quality sleep and drink plenty of water too.

400ml nut milk

40g cooked rice (page 38)

handful of fresh or frozen strawberries

1 scoop of vanilla protein powder

1 tsp vanilla powder

LIFT IT SESSION

Do 45 seconds on, 15 seconds rest x 5 rounds. Or grab some weights and do 1 minute for each with 1 minute of rest in between.

- Kettlebell swings
- Squat and press
- Russian twist
- Wall sit (hold weight out)
- Plank with weighted row

TONICS

Booty burner

Eyes over here! I down this when a beach holiday is fast approaching. It's also a nice accompaniment to a post-workout meal.

Just stir everything together in a jug, then pour into a glass and drink up.

150ml filtered water

juice of 1 grapefruit

juice of 1 lemon

1 tbsp honey or maple syrup

1½ tsp L-carnitine

½ tsp cayenne pepper

DAVE'S BOOTY BURNER

This one comes from Dave, my trainer from Metabolic Fitness. You may know of him from my Instagram feed! Perform 12 to 15 reps (each leg) for each exercise with minimal rest one after the other, then rest for 2 minutes after completing all three exercises. Aim to complete 4 rounds.

- Single leg glute bridge
- Curtsy lunge
- Split squat

Horse it down

I regularly suffer from sore throats from talking too much, although my mother would probably say it's from walking around with wet hair. Try this tonic to help ease and soothe a scratchy, hoarse throat.

Put the water, turmeric, ginger and cinnamon stick in a small saucepan and bring to a gentle simmer, but don't boil. Remove the pan from the heat, cover it and steep for 10 minutes. Strain the tea and stir in the manuka honey. Serve warm with one or two lemon slices and pop the cinnamon stick and a slice of ginger back into the mug.

250ml filtered water

2.5cm piece of fresh turmeric, scrubbed and sliced

2.5cm piece of fresh ginger, peeled and sliced

1 cinnamon stick

1 tbsp manuka honey

1–2 lemon slices, to serve

Morning Tonic

My morning ritual to boost energy, aid digestion and cleanse in seconds – I swear by this tonic. You can add a teaspoon of honey if you need the extra sweetness, but I'm pretty hard core and I just down it.

Pour the water into a mug, then stir in the lemon juice, vinegar and honey (if using) and drink warm.

150ml warm filtered water

juice of ½ lemon

1 tbsp raw unfiltered apple cider vinegar

1 tsp honey (*optional*)

3.
Breakfast

Breakfast cookies

If I could have cookies for every meal, I would, which is why I created this breakfast cookie. It's a simple cookie packed full of all your morning essentials that you can take with you to eat on the go.

Preheat the oven to 180°C. Line a baking tray with non-stick baking paper.

Start by melting the coconut oil in a small pot set over a low heat.

Mash the banana in a medium-sized bowl until it's really smooth, with no visible pieces. Stir in the melted coconut oil, maple syrup and almond butter to create a thick, smooth batter. Add the oats, raisins and chia seeds (if using) until all the oats are covered in the mix. The dough should be thick and sticky.

Divide the dough into six equal portions and roll into balls between the palms of your hands. Place on the lined baking tray and press down each ball into a cookie shape until it's roughly 1.25cm high.

Bake in the preheated oven for 12 to 15 minutes, until the cookies are golden, toasted and firm. Let them cool a little, then serve with a tall glass of cold almond milk.

1 tbsp coconut oil

1 banana, peeled

2 tbsp maple syrup

2 tbsp crunchy almond butter

100g rolled oats

25g raisins

1 tbsp chia seeds (*optional*)

almond milk, to serve

Blueberry breakfast bars

Please give this recipe a go. It has all the ingredients you would usually shove into a bowl of porridge, but it tastes like a fantastic cake bar. Swoon! It's also great to have as a snack during the day.

Preheat the oven to 200°C. Grease a 1lb loaf tin with a little olive oil and line it with non-stick baking paper.

Start by milling the oats into a flour by whizzing them in a blender. Tip the oat flour into a medium-sized bowl and combine with the ground almonds, milled flaxseeds and baking powder.

Zest half the lemon, then squeeze the whole thing. Add the zest and juice to the dry ingredients along with the maple syrup, olive oil and almond milk and stir until a dough forms, then fold in the blueberries. Transfer to the prepared loaf tin, pressing the dough down to make sure the top is even.

Bake in the preheated oven for 20 minutes, until firm and lightly golden along the edges. Cool in the tin for 10 minutes before turning out onto a cutting board and slicing into 10 bars. You can store any leftovers in an airtight container for up to a week.

olive oil, for greasing

120g porridge oats

125g ground almonds

1 tbsp milled flaxseeds

1 tsp baking powder

1 lemon

4 tbsp maple syrup or honey

2 tbsp olive oil

2 tbsp unsweetened almond milk

100g frozen blueberries

These muffins and the ones opposite are both handy on-the-go breakfast options, plus you can alter them to fit your needs. For example, you could leave out some of the egg yolks and add extra whites or you could halve the recipe if you want. I usually have two or three muffins for breakfast or I might take one with me as a snack.

Egg muffins with smoked salmon, feta + cherry tomatoes

Preheat the oven to 200°C. If you're not using a silicone muffin tray, grease a regular muffin tin with coconut oil.

Using a fork, whisk the eggs in a large bowl. Stir in the rest of the ingredients and season with salt and pepper to taste, giving it a good arm workout to make sure the ingredients don't separate. Pour into the muffin moulds until each cup is three-quarters full – you should get about 10 muffins.

Bake in the preheated oven for 25 minutes, until fully cooked through and set. Let any leftover muffins cool fully before placing them in an airtight container to store in the fridge for up to three days. If you store them before they have fully cooled they will go soggy, and no one likes soggy egg muffins! You can reheat them in a low oven, but they taste pretty good cold too.

coconut oil, for greasing (*optional*)

8 eggs

300g grated sweet potato (*optional*)

200g smoked salmon or shredded cooked chicken

30g feta cheese, cut into small cubes

4 cherry tomatoes, quartered

handful of baby spinach, finely chopped

2 tsp chopped fresh flat-leaf parsley

salt and freshly ground black pepper

Egg muffins with chicken, feta + basil

Preheat the oven to 200°C. If you're not using a silicone muffin tray, grease a regular muffin tin with coconut oil.

Using a fork, whisk the egg whites with the whole eggs (if using) in a large bowl, then stir in the apple and basil. Pour into the muffin moulds until each cup is three-quarters full – you should get about 10 muffins. Scatter some feta and chicken into each cup.

Bake in the preheated oven for 20 minutes, until fully cooked through and set. Serve with a little nut butter spread on top.

coconut oil, for greasing (*optional*)

10 egg whites (keep the yolks to make the green mayo on page 34)

2 eggs (*optional*)

1 apple, grated

handful of fresh basil, roughly chopped

100g feta cheese, cut into small cubes

50g leftover shredded cooked chicken

nut butter, to serve

Easy oat scones

I find myself making this recipe all the time. It's so easy and I just use whatever ingredients I have in my press. Sometimes I make these savoury by taking out the blueberries and adding sun-dried tomatoes or feta and some dried Italian herbs. Make the basic recipe once and then play around with different versions to suit your own taste buds or whatever you have on hand.

Preheat the oven to 180°C. Line a baking tray with non-stick baking paper.

Put the oats in a food processor and blitz them into a flour. Tip the oat flour into a medium-sized bowl, then add the baking powder and stir to combine. Spoon in the coconut oil and use your fingertips to rub it into the flour.

Put the bananas, egg whites and honey in the food processor and blend until smooth. Pour into the bowl with the oat flour and stir to combine into a thick, heavy batter, making sure there are no lumps. Toss in the blueberries and give it another quick stir.

Using a dessertspoon, scoop large spoonfuls of the batter onto the lined tray, making five mounds. Alternatively, you could shape these using a scone cutter if you roll the dough in some extra oat flour, but I don't bother because it takes more time!

Bake in the preheated oven for 20 minutes, until light golden around the edges. Let the scones cool for 5 minutes, then serve warm, ideally spread with some peanut butter and topped with chia jam. Let any leftovers cool fully on a wire rack before storing in an airtight container for up to four days.

350g porridge oats

1½ tsp baking powder

3 tbsp coconut oil

2 large ripe bananas, peeled

2 egg whites

2 tbsp honey

125g frozen blueberries

peanut butter, to serve (*optional*)

chia jam (page 75), to serve
    (*optional*)

Peanut butter + raspberry oat scones

One of the most popular posts on my blog is my recipe for peanut butter and raspberry bread. It's pretty fantastic and you should check it out, but I wanted to make a quicker, portion-controlled version, so here it is.

Preheat the oven to 180°C. Line a baking tray with non-stick baking paper.

Start by melting the coconut oil in a small pot set over a low heat.

Put the oats in a food processor or blender (a NutriBullet works well) and blitz them into a flour. Tip the oat flour into a medium-sized bowl, then add the baking powder and stir to combine.

Place the bananas in a separate bowl and mash them really well, until there are no large pieces visible. Stir in the melted coconut oil, peanut butter and maple syrup and mix to combine. Scrape this banana mixture into the oat flour and stir until well combined – the dough will be thick and a little dry at this point – then fold in the raspberries.

Using your hands, form the dough into eight scones and place them on the lined baking tray. Bake in the preheated oven for 20 minutes, until the scones are golden brown and sound hollow when you tap one on the bottom. Let the scones cool for 5 minutes, then serve warm. Let any leftovers cool fully on a wire rack before storing in an airtight container for up to four days.

2 tbsp coconut oil

200g porridge oats

½ tsp baking powder

3 large ripe bananas, peeled

4 tbsp smooth or crunchy peanut butter (I like to use crunchy)

2 tbsp maple syrup or honey

125g fresh raspberries

Brainstorm bowl

I like to add my supplements to raw breakfasts like this one. Try adding some gingko for a busy day or even some omega oils.

Put the walnuts, protein powder, coconut milk and coconut oil in a blender and blitz until smooth. There will be tiny traces of walnut, but that's okay. Pour into a bowl and stir in the chia seeds and desiccated coconut. Place in the fridge for 20 minutes, until thickened and set, or overnight for tomorrow's breakfast.

Serve with a sliced banana or whatever your favourite toppings are. Hemp seeds, toasted pumpkin seeds or cacao nibs would also be good for some added crunch.

10 raw walnuts

25g strawberry protein powder

200ml coconut milk

1 tbsp coconut oil

1 tbsp chia seeds

1 tbsp desiccated coconut

1 ripe banana, peeled and sliced, to serve

Cheeky chocolate pancakes

I love pancakes for breakfast, and when you find that perfect, simple pancake recipe that delivers on taste and texture, it's one you tend to always go back to. The two recipes I chose for this book – these cheeky chocolate pancakes and the skinny crêpes on page 70 – are the only two you'll need to feed your pancake cravings!

Put the egg, cacao powder, almond butter and honey in a small bowl and use a fork to stir everything together until you have a smooth batter.

Heat the oil in a non-stick frying pan set over a high heat, then wipe out any excess with a piece of kitchen paper – you want only a thin film of oil in the base of the pan. Pour 2 tablespoons of the batter into the pan for each pancake. Reduce the heat to medium and cook for 1 minute before flipping each pancake over and cooking for 30 to 40 seconds more. Try not to overcook them, as you want them to be nice and fudgy in the middle.

Serve in a stack drizzled with chocolate sauce and scattered with hemp seeds and fresh raspberries.

1 egg
1 tbsp raw cacao powder
1 tbsp almond butter
2 tsp honey or maple syrup
1 tsp olive oil
chocolate sauce (page 35),
    to serve
hemp seeds, to serve
fresh raspberries, to serve

Skinny crêpes

Growing up, I was more excited about Pancake Tuesday than Christmas. My mum is a crêpe master, so to say I spend countless hours experimenting with healthy crêpe ideas is an understatement.

Put the oats, egg whites and sweetener in a blender (a NutriBullet works well) and blitz until completely smooth.

Heat the oil in a non-stick frying pan set over a medium heat, then wipe out any excess with a piece of kitchen paper – you want only a thin film of oil in the base of the pan. Pour one-third of the batter into the pan and quickly swirl it around to cover the base of the pan in a thin layer. The crêpe will cook fast, so once you see the edges start to lift up, flip it over and cook for 30 seconds on the other side. Slide the crêpe out onto a plate and repeat with the remaining batter.

Serve warm with a squeeze of fresh grapefruit, lemon or lime juice or with your favourite nut butter, homemade Notella or chocolate sauce. Or try something completely different and have a combination of the two: I like my crêpes spread with chocolate sauce and topped with pink grapefruit segments and chopped walnuts.

30g porridge oats

5 egg whites

1 tsp honey, maple syrup or
   stevia powder

1 tsp olive or coconut oil

TOPPINGS:
• fresh grapefruit
• lemon or lime wedges
• nut butter
• homemade Notella (page 35) or chocolate sauce (page 35)

Sweet potato waffles with quick beans

Who else grew up with potato waffles and beans as a staple meal? My mum will kill me for admitting that! It always reminds me of teenage tantrums and college evenings, and guess what? I still crave it now and again, but this version tastes a million times better with added honest goodness.

Mix together the grated sweet potato, eggs, savoury spice, garlic powder and a pinch of salt and pepper in a large bowl.

Grease a waffle iron with a little olive oil and heat it up, then wipe out any excess oil with a piece of kitchen paper – you want only a thin film of oil in the iron. When it's ready to go, spoon 2 tablespoons of the batter into the middle of the waffle iron and spread it out into a square shape using the back of the spoon. Lower the lid and cook for 4 to 5 minutes, until the waffle lifts cleanly off the iron. Repeat with the remaining batter. The waffles will be a little ragged around the edges as opposed to a perfect square, but that's fine.

The key to perfect poached eggs is to first make sure that your eggs are very fresh. Fill a saucepan until the water is about 10cm deep and bring to a steady simmer, then add a few drops of vinegar. Crack each egg into a separate small cup. This is where the fun starts! Create a whirlpool in the saucepan with a slotted spoon and gently slide one egg at a time into the centre. Cook for 3 minutes, or longer if you don't like your yolks runny. Gently lift out with a slotted spoon and set aside to drain on a plate lined with kitchen paper while you cook the beans.

Put all the ingredients for the quick beans in a small pot and set it over a high heat. Bring to the boil, then reduce the heat and simmer for 5 minutes. Spoon the beans on top of the waffles, then add a poached egg on top of each one. Garnish with the parsley, crack over a little black pepper and serve hot.

1 large sweet potato or ½ butternut squash, peeled and grated

2 eggs

1 tbsp ground cumin, ground coriander, dried oregano or whatever your favourite savoury spice is

1 tsp garlic powder

salt and freshly ground black pepper

olive oil, for greasing

1 tsp chopped fresh flat-leaf parsley, to garnish

FOR THE POACHED EGGS:

a few drops of vinegar (I use apple cider vinegar)

4 eggs

FOR THE BEANS:

1 x 400g tin of haricot beans, drained and rinsed

200g tomato passata

1 tbsp apple cider vinegar

1 tbsp honey or maple syrup

1 tsp dried Italian herbs

1 tsp paprika

1 tsp tomato purée

1 tsp tamari or soy sauce

Peanut butter + jam sambos

Eh, yes to having this for breakfast every morning! I used to despise peanut butter, but after my stint modelling in New York I realized that a peanut butter and jam sandwich is like tea: it solves everything.

Start by making the chia jam. Put the raspberries in a microwave-safe bowl and cook on a high heat for 60 seconds, until they have broken down. Mash them with a fork, then stir in the chia seeds and honey. Set aside for 15 to 20 minutes, until the jam has thickened up.

Now let's make the all-important sandwich base. Put the oats in a blender (a NutriBullet works well) and blitz into a flour. Add the eggs, peanut butter, yogurt and baking powder and blend into a smooth batter.

Melt a little coconut oil in a non-stick frying pan set over a high heat. Pour 3 tablespoons of the batter into the centre of the pan and use the back of the spoon to spread into a square shape. Cook for 2 to 3 minutes, until the sides easily lift off the pan. Flip over, lower the heat to medium and cook for a further 3 minutes. Transfer to a plate and repeat with the remaining batter until you have 10 'slices' of bread. If you have a big pan, you can make two at a time.

Once all the bread is made, slather the jam, which should be pretty thick by now, over half the slices and sandwich together with the remaining bread. To add another dimension, add some sliced banana and peanut butter too.

90g porridge oats

4 eggs

2 tbsp smooth or crunchy peanut butter

2 tbsp Greek yogurt

½ tsp baking powder

coconut oil, for cooking

FOR THE CHIA JAM:

60g fresh raspberries or your favourite berry

1½ tbsp chia seeds

2 tsp honey

OPTIONAL ADD-INS:
• 1 ripe banana, peeled and sliced
• smooth or crunchy peanut butter

Bacon + avocado breakfast wrap

Yes, this wrap can cure hangovers. I don't want to excite you, but it may be the answer to a healthier, more satisfying alternative to the breakfast roll.

Put the eggs, flaxseeds and a pinch of salt in a blender and blitz until smooth.

Melt a little coconut oil in a non-stick frying pan set over a medium-high heat. Pour the egg mixture into the pan and quickly swirl it around to cover the base. Cook for 3 minutes, until the edges are starting to lift up and the base is firm enough to flip. Turn over and cook for 1 minute more, then slide out onto a plate.

Use the same pan to cook the bacon until it's cooked through and crisp.

Spread the pesto and then the mashed avocado on one side of the egg wrap. Top with the cooked bacon, baby spinach and beans. Roll up tightly and slice in half to serve.

2 eggs
2 tbsp milled flaxseeds
pinch of sea salt
coconut oil, for cooking

FOR THE FILLING:
1 slice of bacon, fat trimmed off
1 tbsp basil or sun-dried tomato
    pesto (page 32)
¼ ripe avocado, peeled, stoned
    and mashed
handful of baby spinach
2 tbsp tinned beans of your
    choice, drained and rinsed

If you need something to brighten up your mornings, these two chia puddings will definitely do just that. Even if you're a fan of chia it can get a little boring, so switch it up and get creative with different flavours. These are my favourites.

| SERVES 1 |

Lemon + coconut chia pudding

First zest half the lemon, then squeeze the whole thing. Put the zest and juice in a small bowl with the coconut milk, honey and turmeric and whisk until the milk turns yellow, then stir in the chia seeds and yogurt. Place in the fridge for 20 minutes, until thickened and set, or overnight for tomorrow's breakfast.

1 lemon
150ml coconut milk
1 tbsp honey or maple syrup
1 tsp ground turmeric
3 tbsp chia seeds
1 tbsp coconut yogurt or your
    favourite yogurt

| SERVES 1 |

Berry chia pudding

Put the berries, almond milk, honey, orange zest and vanilla (if using) in a blender and blitz until smooth, then pour into a jar or glass and stir in the chia seeds. Place in the fridge for 20 minutes, until thickened and set, or overnight for tomorrow's breakfast. Serve with a dollop of your favourite yogurt on top.

2 handfuls of fresh or frozen
    berries
150ml unsweetened almond
    milk
1 tbsp honey or maple syrup
1 tbsp orange zest (optional)
1 tsp vanilla powder or 1 vanilla
    pod, cut in half lengthways and
    seeds scraped out (optional)
2 tbsp chia seeds
your favourite probiotic yogurt,
    to serve

Carrot cake porridge

I like to add egg whites for a boost of protein in my porridge, but you could use rice, pea, hemp or whey protein powder instead.

Put the oats and almond milk in a small saucepan set over a medium heat and cook, stirring regularly, until the porridge has a thick, almost stodgy consistency. Remove from the heat and use a fork to whisk in the egg whites until the porridge is slightly fluffy and creamy, then stir in the carrot, flaxseeds, vanilla powder, sweetener and cinnamon. If you like your porridge a little runnier, add the remaining 50ml of almond milk.

Transfer to a bowl and serve hot with the dates, carrot, chia jam and almond butter on top. Or if you want to take things up a notch, stuff the dates with the almond butter and chia jam and serve them that way (which also makes a great snack too).

30g porridge oats

200–250ml unsweetened almond milk

2 egg whites

1 small carrot, peeled and grated

1 tsp milled flaxseeds

1 tsp vanilla powder

1 tsp honey, maple syrup or stevia powder

½ tsp ground cinnamon

TOPPINGS:
- 3 Medjool dates, pitted and sliced
- ¼ carrot, peeled and grated
- 1 tbsp chia jam (page 75)
- 1 tbsp almond butter

BANANA BREAD
PORRIDGE

POST-WORKOUT
PORRIDGE

CHOCOLATE CHIP
PORRIDGE

CARROT CAKE
PORRIDGE

SAVOURY PORRIDGE
WITH BACON,
AVOCADO +
PARMESAN

Chocolate chip porridge

You may have figured out by now that I'm a fan of dessert-type foods for breakfast. Mornings are hard enough as they are – something sweet makes them far more manageable!

Put the oats and 200ml of the almond milk in a small saucepan set over a medium heat and cook, stirring regularly, until the porridge has a thick, almost stodgy consistency. Remove from the heat and use a fork to whisk in the egg whites until the porridge is slightly fluffy and creamy, then stir in the cacao powder and nibs, vanilla powder and honey. If you like your porridge a little runnier, add the remaining 50ml of almond milk.

Transfer to a bowl and serve hot with the fresh blackberries, grapefruit segments, dark chocolate shavings, bee pollen and coconut flakes on top.

30g porridge oats

200–250ml unsweetened
  almond milk

2 egg whites

1 tbsp raw cacao powder

2 tsp cacao nibs

1 tsp vanilla powder

1 tsp honey, maple syrup or
  stevia powder

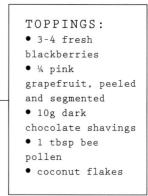

```
TOPPINGS:
• 3-4 fresh
blackberries
• ¼ pink
grapefruit, peeled
and segmented
• 10g dark
chocolate shavings
• 1 tbsp bee
pollen
• coconut flakes
```

Banana bread porridge

I always get asked what my favourite comfort food is. When I say it's porridge – a warm bowl of nostalgic bliss – most people are a little underwhelmed by my response, but they've obviously never pimped up their porridge like this!

Put the oats and almond milk in a small saucepan set over a medium heat and cook, stirring regularly, until the porridge has a thick, almost stodgy consistency. Remove from the heat and stir in the mashed banana until the porridge is creamy, then stir in the walnuts, vanilla powder, mixed spice and sweetener. If you like your porridge a little runnier, add the remaining 50ml of almond milk.

Transfer to a bowl and serve hot with the sliced banana and kiwi, a spoonful of chocolate sauce and some cacao nibs on top.

30g porridge oats

200–250ml unsweetened almond milk

1 small ripe banana, peeled and mashed really well

1 tbsp chopped walnuts

1 tsp vanilla powder

1 tsp mixed spice

1 tsp honey, maple syrup or stevia powder

TOPPINGS:
- 1 ripe banana, peeled and sliced
- 1 kiwi, halved or peeled and sliced
- chocolate sauce (page 35)
- cacao nibs

Post-workout porridge

Breakfast, lunch or dinner, this one's always a winner . . . okay, I'll stop now. But on a serious note, it's the perfect post-workout meal in minutes.

Put the oats and 200ml of the almond milk in a small saucepan set over a medium heat and cook, stirring regularly, until the porridge has a thick, almost stodgy consistency. Remove from the heat and use a fork to whisk in the egg whites until the porridge is slightly fluffy and creamy, then stir in the vanilla and sweetener. If you like your porridge a little runnier, add the remaining 50ml of almond milk.

Transfer to a bowl and serve hot with a dollop of Greek yogurt, some fresh berries and a little torn fresh mint on top.

30g porridge oats

200–250ml unsweetened almond milk

2 egg whites

1 tsp vanilla powder or extract

1 tsp honey, maple syrup or stevia powder

TOPPINGS:
- Greek yogurt
- fresh berries
- fresh mint leaves

WORK THE MIDDLE

Do 45 seconds on each one then 15 seconds off x 4 rounds.

- Toe taps
- Leg raises
- Russian twists
- Plank

Savoury porridge with bacon, avocado + Parmesan

You're probably wondering how this came about. I've always used oats as a risotto substitute, so a savoury bowl of porridge wasn't a huge stretch from that. If you like savoury brekkies but are tired of everyday eggs, give this a go.

Put the egg in a saucepan and add enough cold water to cover it by 2.5cm. Bring to the boil, then remove from the heat, cover the pan and let the egg sit in the hot water for 12 minutes. Remove the egg from the water with a slotted spoon and run under cold water to cool it down. When it's cool enough to handle, peel the egg and cut it in half.

Meanwhile, if you're using the bacon, set a frying pan over a medium heat. Put the bacon in the pan and cook until crisp, then use a slotted spoon to transfer the bacon to a plate lined with kitchen paper to soak up any excess grease.

Put the oats in a small saucepan set over a medium heat and toast them for a few minutes, then pour in the nut milk or vegetable stock. Once the liquid starts to simmer, add the spinach and cook, stirring regularly, until the spinach has wilted and the porridge has a thick, almost stodgy consistency. Remove from the heat and stir in the cooked bacon or the sun-dried tomatoes, Parmesan shavings, spices or herbs and the tamari.

Transfer to a bowl and serve hot with the hardboiled egg and avocado slices on top, then garnish with some fresh parsley.

1 egg
1 slice of bacon, diced, or 4 sun-dried tomatoes in oil, drained and chopped
40g porridge oats
300ml nut milk, such as unsweetened almond milk, or vegetable stock
handful of baby spinach
2 tbsp Parmesan cheese shavings or nutritional yeast
1 tbsp savoury spices or herbs, such as dried Italian herbs, paprika or dried thyme
1 tsp tamari or soy sauce
½ ripe avocado, peeled, stoned and sliced
chopped fresh flat-leaf parsley, to garnish

N'oats bowl

I'm not dissing oats here – I love them – but if you're looking to dodge the stodge, why not give this a try?

Place the egg whites in a spotlessly clean, dry bowl and whisk until stiff.

Pour the almond milk into a small saucepan and set it over a medium heat. Once the milk starts to simmer, stir in the coconut flour and keep stirring until the mix begins to thicken to a creamy sauce consistency. Add the cacao powder, sweetener and flaxseeds and stir until it thickens slightly more. Fold in the egg whites and cook for 1 minute.

Transfer to a bowl and serve hot with a raw cookie dough ball, some chocolate squares, fresh berries and seeds on top, then drizzle with the chocolate sauce.

2 egg whites

200ml unsweetened almond milk

20g coconut flour

1½ tbsp raw cacao powder

1 tbsp honey, maple syrup or stevia powder

1½ tsp milled flaxseeds

```
TOPPINGS:
• 1 raw cookie
dough ball (page
216)
• a few squares
of dark chocolate,
roughly chopped
• handful of fresh
berries
• 1 tbsp hemp and/
or sunflower seeds
• 1 tbsp chocolate
sauce (page 35)
```

COOKIE
DOUGH BALL

If you like your overnight oats on the stodgy side, only use 200ml nut milk or just add an extra tablespoon of oats. Adding some milled flaxseeds or whole chia seeds would thicken it up too.

| SERVES 1 |

Strawberries + cream overnight oats

Place the oats, almond milk, yogurt and honey in a bowl and stir to combine, then stir in the strawberries. Pour into a jar, screw on the lid and place in the fridge to set overnight.

45g porridge oats
200–250ml unsweetened
    almond milk (see the note above)
1 tbsp Greek yogurt
1–2 tsp honey or maple syrup
handful of fresh strawberries,
    hulled and diced

| SERVES 1 |

Notella overnight oats

Put the hazelnut milk, cacao powder and honey in a bowl and stir until the cacao and honey have dissolved into the milk. Stir in the oats and cacao nibs, then pour into a jar, screw on the lid and place in the fridge to set overnight.

200–250ml hazelnut milk (see
    the note above)
1 tbsp raw cacao powder
1 tbsp honey or maple syrup
45g porridge oats
1 tbsp cacao nibs

Quick savoury granola

We're all fans of that one staple granola recipe we have up our sleeve, but even the homemade versions are pretty sweet and I don't know when to stop picking and nibbling my way through the container – hence the creation of a savoury granola. It's perfect for sprinkling on eggs, soups and salads or simply served with some Greek yogurt.

Set a frying pan over a medium-high heat. Once the pan is hot, pour in the oil and let it heat up, then toss in the oats, seeds and nuts. Stir constantly for 7 to 8 minutes, until everything is nicely toasted. The seeds will pop, so watch out you don't get any in the face!

Add the spices and stir to combine, then add the tamari and cook, still stirring, for another 2 minutes. By now the granola should be golden and toasted all over and the seeds and nuts should be super crunchy – have a little taste to check. Remove from the heat and stir in the nutritional yeast and a pinch of salt.

Let the granola cool completely before storing in an airtight container for up to three weeks.

1 tbsp olive oil

200g jumbo oats

100g mixed seeds

60g cashews, roughly chopped

1 tsp cayenne pepper

¾ tsp ground turmeric

½ tsp smoked paprika

3 tbsp tamari or soy sauce

3 tbsp nutritional yeast

pinch of sea salt

On-the-go sweet potato egg pots

These sweet potato pots are like a healthy hash brown cradling some serious yolk porn!

Preheat the oven to 200°C. Grease a six-hole muffin tin with a little olive or coconut oil.

Put the sweet potato in a medium-sized bowl along with one egg, the dried herbs, ground black pepper and lemon zest (if using) and stir to combine.

Divide the mixture into six equal portions. Take one portion and press it onto the base and up the sides of one hole of the muffin tin to make a nest. Repeat with the remaining sweet potato mixture. Bake in the preheated oven for 8 to 10 minutes, until tender.

Remove the tin from the oven. Crack one egg into each sweet potato nest, then scatter over the feta. Return to the oven and bake for 10 minutes more, until the eggs are set. Garnish with small sprigs of fresh thyme and serve warm for breakfast, or let them cool before packing as a snack or have two with some leafy greens as a lunchtime salad.

olive or coconut oil, for greasing

1 large sweet potato, peeled and grated

7 eggs

1 tsp dried Italian herbs

1 tsp ground black pepper

zest of 1 lemon (*optional*)

60g feta cheese, cut into small cubes

small sprigs of fresh thyme, to garnish

Post-workout omelette

This is my typical breakfast on a weekday, as it's perfect after training or to fuel you for the day ahead. It's a recipe I always come back to because it's so satisfying and keeps the hunger away, plus it has a nice mix of protein and carbohydrate, which is exactly what you need after a gym session to rebuild and restore so that you are ready to go for round two tomorrow. Don't forget that your body metabolizes carbohydrates best after a workout, so don't neglect your carbs!

Melt the coconut oil in a non-stick frying pan set over a high heat. Add the onion and cook for 1 to 2 minutes. Add the sweet potato and spinach and cook, stirring, for 4 to 5 minutes, until the sweet potato is tender and starting to brown a little. Remove half the onion, sweet potato and spinach mixture from the pan onto a plate and set aside.

Return the pan to the heat with half the mix still in it. Pour in the beaten eggs and stir to combine for a moment, then lower the heat to medium and let the bottom cook and firm up. Once the edges start to lift up a little, flip it over and cook for 2 minutes more. Remove the pan from the heat. Top the omelette with the reserved onion, sweet potato and spinach, then scatter over the feta or avocado and the sprouts and coriander. Fold the omelette in half, slide it out onto a plate and serve straight away.

1 tsp coconut oil

½ red onion, peeled and finely diced

80–120g sweet potato, peeled and grated or spiralized

40g baby spinach

3 eggs or 5 egg whites and 1 full egg, beaten

35g feta cheese or ½ ripe avocado, peeled, stoned and diced

1 tbsp sprout mix

1 tsp chopped fresh coriander

BOX HIIT

Do 1 minute for each with 1 minute of rest in between x 5 rounds.

- Shadow box (with light weights for a more intense burn)
- Skip (high knees for harder version)
- Crunches
- Side-to-side shuffle floor taps
- Push-ups

Blueberry, apple + cinnamon sweet omelette

Yep, a sweet omelette. Eggs are the most versatile food on the planet, so why can't they be sweet? I know this is in the breakfast chapter, but it's also a nice quick dessert to whip up when you're craving something sweet in the evening, which is me every night. You can also make a savoury 'pizza' version of this omelette – just leave out the honey and swap the fruit for some feta and pepperoni and finish with a dollop of pesto. Epic!

Preheat the oven to 190°C.

Put the egg whites in a spotlessly clean, dry bowl and whisk until stiff.

Put the egg yolks, lemon juice, yogurt, honey and cinnamon in a separate bowl and mix until well combined. Fold in the egg whites a little at a time, trying not to overmix.

Melt the coconut oil in a non-stick ovenproof frying pan set over a medium-high heat. Pour in the egg mixture and quickly swirl it around to cover the base of the pan. Cook for 3 to 4 minutes, until the base and edges are starting to get firm, before sprinkling over the blueberries and scattering over the apple slices (if using).

Transfer to the preheated oven and bake for 15 minutes, until the omelette has puffed up and the edges are nice and crispy. Slide the omelette out onto a plate, scatter with some toasted flaked almonds and serve straight away with an extra dollop of Greek yogurt on top.

3 eggs, separated
juice of ½ lemon
2 tbsp Greek yogurt, plus extra
   to serve
1–2 tsp honey
pinch of ground cinnamon
1 tsp coconut oil
handful of fresh or frozen
   blueberries
½ apple or pear, thinly sliced
   (*optional*)
toasted flaked almonds, to serve

Green eggs with spicy nut sauce

My two favourite things in one recipe: eggs and nuts! I know that the combination of nut butter and eggs sounds strange. Sometimes I mention it and people gasp in horror, but don't knock it till you've tried it! One of my all-time favourite snacks is halved boiled eggs with a tablespoon of almond butter in the middle – check out the recipe on page 136.

Start with the spicy nut sauce: just whisk together all the ingredients in a small glass or bowl and set aside.

Put the eggs and cottage cheese in a small bowl and whisk together.

Heat the oil or butter in a non-stick frying pan set over a medium heat, then add the garlic and reduce the heat to low so that it doesn't burn. Cook for a few seconds, then add the spinach and cook for 2 to 3 minutes, until it has wilted right down. Pour in the egg and cottage cheese mixture and cook, stirring continuously, for 2 to 3 minutes, until the eggs are just cooked through – try not to overcook the eggs here or they will be tough and rubbery.

Transfer to a plate and serve the spicy nut sauce alongside. Sprinkle with the chopped fresh herbs and a pinch of toasted sesame seeds (or your favourite seeds) for some extra crunch.

2 eggs

1 tbsp cottage cheese

1 tsp olive or coconut oil or butter

1 small garlic clove, peeled and crushed

60g baby spinach, roughly chopped

handful of fresh parsley or coriander, chopped, to garnish

toasted sesame seeds, to serve

FOR THE SPICY NUT SAUCE:

1½ tbsp peanut or almond butter

1 tsp honey

½ tsp chilli powder

¼ tsp cayenne pepper

4.

Lunch

Spicy bean + bulgur soup

Hands up if you're like me and sometimes think that soup needs some extra oomph and bite. I created this soup during the winter, when I needed a handy lunch, a warm dish full of flavour and something that would leave me satisfied and would clear my sinuses to boot.

Heat the oil in a pot set over a medium heat. Add the onions (keep a few thinly sliced rings back for garnish if you want), cover the pot with a lid and sweat for 5 to 6 minutes, until the onions have softened.

Meanwhile, put the tomatoes, red peppers, most of the chillies (keep a few slices back for garnish), garlic, tamari, vinegar, tomato purée, spices and some salt and pepper in a blender and blitz until smooth.

Pour the tomato mixture into the pot with the onions. Add the cooked bulgur, beans and stock and bring to the boil. Cover the pot with a lid, reduce the heat and simmer the soup for 15 minutes.

Ladle into warmed bowls and serve with the diced avocado, the reserved onion and chilli and a drizzle of hot sauce on top.

2 tbsp olive oil

2 red onions, peeled and cut into large pieces

8 ripe tomatoes, halved

2 red peppers, deseeded and chopped

2 fresh red chillies, deseeded and thinly sliced

2 garlic cloves, peeled and chopped

2 tbsp tamari or soy sauce

1 tbsp apple cider vinegar

1 tbsp tomato purée

2 tsp ground cumin

2 tsp ground coriander

1 tsp cayenne pepper

1 tsp ground cinnamon

salt and freshly ground black pepper

600g cooked bulgur (page 36) or rice (page 38)

1 x 400g tin of black beans, drained and rinsed

1 x 400g tin of beans of your choice, drained and rinsed

1 litre vegetable stock

1 ripe avocado, peeled, stoned and diced, to serve

hot sauce, to serve

Carrot + cannellini bean soup

Carrot is my favourite veg, hands down. Most of my friends have called me Bugs Bunny at some point while I loudly munch on a raw carrot. I love them because they're so versatile, from carrot mash to soup or even croutons.

Heat the olive oil in a large pot set over a medium-high heat. Add the carrots and cook for 5 minutes, stirring every minute so that they brown evenly. Stir in the maple syrup, harissa and cinnamon and cook for 2 minutes before pouring in 600ml of the hot stock and the beans. Season with some salt and pepper, cover the pot with a lid, lower the heat and simmer for 10 minutes.

Pour the soup into a blender or use a hand-held blender and blitz until smooth. Check the consistency – if you want the soup to be thinner, add the remaining 200ml of the stock and blend again.

Ladle into warmed bowls and garnish with a pinch of caraway seeds in each bowl.

1 tbsp olive oil

6 carrots, peeled and finely diced

1 tbsp maple syrup

1½ tsp harissa (red curry paste works well too)

¼ tsp ground cinnamon

600–800ml hot vegetable stock

1 x 400g tin of cannellini beans, drained and rinsed

salt and freshly ground black pepper

pinch of caraway seeds, to garnish

SPICY BEAN
+ BULGUR
SOUP

CREAM OF
ASPARAGUS
SOUP

CARROT +
CANNELLINI
BEAN SOUP

Cream of asparagus soup

You can get tons of benefits from this little beaut of a veg – for starters, asparagus has great anti-inflammatory and antioxidant properties. If you find it a challenge to get your greens in, try this soup.

Preheat the grill to high.

Snap the woody ends off the asparagus and put the spears on a baking tray. Drizzle with 1 tablespoon of the olive oil, season with salt and pepper and pop the tray under the grill for about 15 minutes, until the asparagus is tender.

Meanwhile, heat the remaining tablespoon of oil in a pot set over a medium heat. Add the onion, cover the pot with a lid and sweat for 5 to 6 minutes, until the onion has softened. Add the garlic and cook for 1 minute, just until it's fragrant, then add the roasted asparagus and its juices along with the peas, fresh herbs and stock. Remove from the heat and purée until smooth with a hand-held blender, then put the pot back over a medium heat and stir in the coconut milk.

Let the soup simmer for 1 or 2 minutes to reheat, then ladle into warmed bowls. Garnish with a swirl of yogurt and a fresh coriander leaf in each bowl and serve straight away.

600g asparagus
2 tbsp olive oil
salt and freshly ground black pepper
1 onion, peeled and diced
1 garlic clove, peeled and chopped
200g frozen peas
8 fresh basil leaves
6 fresh mint leaves
600ml vegetable stock
1 x 400ml tin of full-fat
    coconut milk
Greek yogurt, to garnish
fresh coriander leaves, to garnish

Miso, mushroom + chickpea soup

You can never have too many recipes for mushroom soup. It's one of those soups that if it's on a menu, I'm getting it! This one is a nice light version, but it's still as tasty and creamy as ever.

Preheat the grill to high.

Whisk the miso and olive oil together in a small bowl. Rub the paste on the mushrooms, then place them on a baking tray and pop them under the grill for about 15 minutes, until the mushrooms are tender.

Meanwhile, put the diced onion in a pot with a little water, cover the pot with a lid and sweat for 5 to 6 minutes, until the onion has softened. Add the garlic and cook for 1 minute, just until it's fragrant, then add the stock, thyme and some salt and pepper. Bring to the boil, then remove the pot from the heat and add the grilled mushrooms and their juices along with the chickpeas. Blitz with a hand-held blender until smooth, then pour in the almond milk and blend again.

Return the pot to the heat for a few minutes to warm up the soup again, then ladle into warmed bowls and serve straight away.

2 tbsp miso paste
2 tbsp olive oil
12 Portobello mushrooms
1 onion, peeled and finely diced
2 garlic cloves, peeled and
    crushed
400ml vegetable stock
1 tbsp fresh thyme leaves
salt and freshly ground black pepper
1 x 400g tin of chickpeas,
    drained and rinsed
300ml unsweetened almond milk

Turkey, squash + kale soup

This is a meal in a soup bowl. It's such a treat when I prep this, as it gets better when you make it ahead of time. It also really energizes me during the day and keeps hunger at bay.

Heat the olive oil in a pot set over a high heat. Add the onion and garlic and let them sizzle for 1 to 2 minutes, stirring constantly so that they don't brown too much. Add the turkey mince and thyme and cook, stirring regularly, for 5 minutes, until browned. Use a wooden spoon to break up the mince, but not too much – you want some small chunks in the soup.

Stir in the celery, squash and tomato purée, then pour in the chicken stock and season with a little salt and pepper. Cover the pot and bring to the boil, then lower the heat and let the soup simmer for 10 minutes. Add the kale and simmer for 5 minutes more, uncovered, until it has softened.

Ladle into warmed bowls and serve straight away.

1 tbsp olive oil

1 red onion, peeled and finely diced

4 garlic cloves, peeled and crushed

600g turkey mince

1 tbsp finely chopped fresh thyme leaves

4 celery stalks, chopped

½ butternut squash, peeled and diced into small chunks

2 tbsp tomato purée

800ml chicken stock

salt and freshly ground black pepper

200g kale, tough ribs removed and leaves roughly chopped

Pho on the go

I hope you appreciate the name of this soup – I had to make a hero pho when I thought of it! I love homemade pho, as it's a great way to use up leftovers and it packs in loads of veggies and fresh herbs. I make pho a lot when I'm gearing up for a holiday or a big shoot, as I find it really fills me up and keeps me from picking at any other nibbles throughout the day.

Put the eggs in a saucepan and add enough cold water to cover them by 2.5cm. Bring to the boil, then remove from the heat, cover the pan and let the eggs sit in the hot water for 12 minutes. Remove the eggs from the water with a slotted spoon and run under cold water to cool them down. When they're cool enough to handle, peel the eggs and cut in half.

Meanwhile, put the onion, garlic, ginger, cinnamon sticks, cloves and chicken stock in a pot. Cover with a lid and bring to the boil, then reduce the heat and simmer for 20 minutes. Remove from the heat and scoop out all the solids with a slotted spoon so that you're left with a clear broth.

Add the spiralized veggie 'noodles', red pepper, cooked chicken, bean sprouts, tamari and vinegar and cook for 1 minute, until the noodles and chicken are heated through.

Ladle into bowls and garnish with the chillies and fresh herbs. Put two egg halves on top of each bowl and serve with lime wedges on the side.

4 eggs

1 large onion, peeled and quartered

2 garlic cloves, peeled and left whole

5cm piece of fresh ginger, cut into a few large pieces

2 cinnamon sticks

2 cloves

1 litre chicken stock

2 large courgettes or ½ peeled butternut squash, spiralized

1 red pepper, thinly sliced

480g cooked shredded chicken

100g bean sprouts

2 tbsp tamari or soy sauce

1½ tsp rice vinegar

2 fresh red chillies, deseeded and thinly sliced

handful of fresh mixed herbs, such as mint, coriander and basil, chopped

2 limes, cut into wedges, to serve

Cabbage wraps

Cabbage wraps can be tricky to fold at first, but I promise that you'll quickly become an expert. It's another thing to add to your CV – you never know when that skill could come in handy! Use Savoy cabbage here for a wider leaf, but if you're daring, try red cabbage. It will stain your fingers and cutting board, but the colour is worth it. These wraps are another handy way to use up all your tasty leftovers.

Start by lightly steaming the cabbage leaves for 5 to 6 minutes, until tender. Transfer to a bowl of ice-cold water to shock them and keep their bright colour, then pat them dry to get rid of the excess liquid.

Spread each cabbage leaf with the hummus, mashed avocado and pesto, or tahini, depending on which wrap you're making. Load up the rest of the fillings along the centre of each leaf and tightly fold it up as you would a regular wrap, securing the bottom. To serve, cut each wrap in half on the diagonal.

FOR THE VEGGIE WRAP:

2 large Savoy or red cabbage leaves

2 tbsp hummus (page 34)

40g cooked quinoa (page 39)

1 roasted sweet potato, flesh
   scooped out and mashed

handful of fresh sprouts

FOR THE TUNACADO WRAP:

2 large Savoy or red cabbage leaves

½ ripe avocado, peeled, stoned
   and mashed

2 tsp pesto (page 32)

1 small tin of tuna, drained

1 small carrot, peeled and grated

handful of baby spinach

FOR THE DINNER WRAP:

2 large Savoy or red cabbage leaves

2 tsp tahini

½ leftover roasted sweet potato,
   flesh scooped out and mashed

handful of cooked shredded chicken

1 tbsp toasted flaked almonds

Green wrap with chicken + Parmesan

This light, vibrant, fluffy, protein-packed wrap base is a great addition to your lunchbox. I love this filling, but use whatever is in your fridge or any leftovers that might be lurking around.

Put the eggs, spinach and herbs in a blender and blitz until smooth.

Heat a thin film of oil in a non-stick frying pan set over a high heat. Pour in the spinach mixture and quickly swirl it around to cover the base of the pan. Lower the heat to medium and cook for 3 to 4 minutes, until the edges are starting to lift up and the base is set. Flip over and cook for 3 minutes on the other side. Remove from the pan and set aside.

Lightly season the chicken strips with some salt and pepper. Using the same pan, fry the chicken for 4 to 5 minutes on each side, until cooked through.

Whisk the lemon juice and tahini together in a glass.

Load up the green wrap with the chicken strips, scatter over the Parmesan shavings, drizzle with the tahini lemon sauce and finish with a pinch of salt and pepper before tightly rolling up and slicing in half on the diagonal.

2 eggs
handful of baby spinach
1 tbsp dried Italian herbs
1 tbsp olive oil
1 small chicken fillet, sliced into
    thin strips
salt and freshly ground black pepper
juice of ½ lemon
1½ tsp tahini
15g Parmesan cheese shavings

The Nelly frittata

Mackerel is one of my favourite foods for adding omegas to a dish. I always have it stocked in my press for a quick nutritious hit.

Preheat the grill to high.

Snap the woody ends off the bottom of each asparagus spear, then cut each spear into bite-sized pieces.

Heat the olive oil in a small ovenproof frying pan set over a high heat. Add the asparagus and cook for 3 to 4 minutes. Lower the heat to medium, add the mackerel and spinach and cook for 1 minute more, until the spinach has wilted. Pour in the beaten eggs and give everything a stir to make sure the asparagus, mackerel and spinach are evenly distributed around the pan, then scatter over the feta and season with a pinch of salt and pepper.

Cook for 3 to 4 minutes before popping the pan under the grill for 5 minutes, until the eggs are cooked through. Slide the frittata out of the pan and cut into wedges. This frittata is good served hot or at room temperature.

6 asparagus spears
1 tbsp olive oil
1 x 125g tin of mackerel, drained
handful of baby spinach
4 eggs, beaten
30g feta cheese, cut into small
   cubes
salt and freshly ground black pepper

Sweet potato sliders

You've probably guessed by now that sweet potatoes are a staple in my kitchen. They're a great way of getting your carbohydrates in and satisfying a sweet tooth. Try these sliders, which you can make sweet or savoury, as a simple alternative to bread.

Preheat the oven to 220°C. Line a baking tray with non-stick baking paper.

Put the sweet potato slices on the lined tray in a single layer. Bake in the preheated oven for 20 minutes, until tender and crispy along the edges. Or you could pop the sweet potato slices in the toaster for a faster option.

Load up the sweet potato thins with your favourite topping combination and enjoy!

1 large sweet potato, cut
   lengthways into slices 1cm thick

AVOCADO + EGG TOPPING:
1 ripe avocado, peeled, stoned
   and mashed
1 hardboiled egg, quartered (see
   the recipe on page 110 for how to
   cook the egg)
salt and freshly ground black pepper

VEGGIE TOPPING:
2 tbsp hummus (page 34)
3 cherry tomatoes, sliced
1 radish, thinly sliced
1 tsp pesto (page 32)
tiny fresh basil leaves, to garnish

CHOCOLATE, FIG + NUT TOPPING:
1 tbsp Notella (page 35)
1 fresh fig, sliced
3 walnuts, chopped
fresh rosemary, to garnish

PEANUT BUTTER + BANANA
TOPPING:
1 tbsp peanut butter
⅓ banana, peeled and sliced
1 tsp chia seeds

Cashew, bean + oat burgers

Making a veggie burger in 30 minutes is harder than you might think, but I was up for the challenge. I spent a lot of time tweaking this recipe, but my sister told me that it's the best vegan burger she's ever had, and she's my toughest critic.

Preheat the oven to 200°C. Line a baking tray with non-stick baking paper.

Put the beans in a food processor and blend until smooth. Add the cashews, pesto, tamari and spices and blend again until almost smooth, with small traces of cashews still visible to add some crunch. Tip into a large bowl and stir in the oats until well combined.

Divide into four portions and roll into balls. Place on the lined tray and press down to form each one into a patty 1.5cm thick.

Bake in the preheated oven for 15 minutes, until the burgers are crispy around the edges. Remove from the oven, flip each burger over and return to the oven to bake for 5 minutes more.

Spread the top half of each burger bun with mashed avocado. Put a little shredded lettuce on the bottom half of each bun, then top with a spoonful of hummus (I like beetroot hummus here) and a burger. Sandwich together with the top half of the bun and skewer with a cocktail stick to keep the burgers together.

1 x 400g tin of mixed beans, drained and rinsed
100g raw cashews
2 tbsp sun-dried tomato pesto (page 32)
2 tbsp tamari or soy sauce
2 tsp ground cumin
1 tsp ground turmeric
6 tbsp porridge oats
4 burger buns, to serve
1 ripe avocado, peeled, stoned and mashed, to serve
shredded lettuce, to serve
hummus (page 34), to serve

Root veg + feta fritters

A crispy root veg fritter with some creamy feta is an epic combination for a satisfying lunch.

Preheat the oven to 200°C.

Pile the grated root veg into the middle of a clean tea towel, gather it up into a ball and squeeze out as much liquid as possible.

Put the eggs, feta, ground almonds, coriander, cumin, cinnamon and some salt and pepper in a large bowl and stir together, then add the grated veg and stir until well combined into a batter.

Heat the olive oil in a frying pan set over a high heat. Pour 1½ tablespoons of the batter into the hot pan for each fritter and cook for 2 minutes before turning over and cooking the other side for 2 minutes more. You can cook a few at a time depending on how big your pan is, but don't overcrowd the pan. Transfer to a baking tray and repeat with the remaining batter, then bake the fritters in the preheated oven for 8 to 10 minutes, until cooked through.

Meanwhile, put the yogurt and lemon juice in a small bowl and whisk together, then stir in the coriander. Serve the fritters with the dip on the side.

400g parsnips, peeled and grated

400g carrots, peeled and grated

1 large sweet potato or purple potato, peeled and grated

3 eggs, beaten

120g feta cheese, cut into small cubes

4 tbsp ground almonds or coconut flour

2 tbsp chopped fresh coriander

2 tsp ground cumin

½ tsp ground cinnamon

salt and freshly ground black pepper

2 tbsp olive oil

FOR THE DIP:

6 tbsp natural yogurt

juice of 1 lemon

handful of fresh coriander, chopped

Asian-style tuna balls

This is my favourite fish recipe and meal prep dish – in fact, it's my favourite hero recipe in the entire book. They're so easy that after you've made them just once, you probably won't even need to follow the recipe again.

Preheat the oven to 200°C. Line a baking tray with non-stick baking paper.

Put all the ingredients for the tuna balls in a large bowl and mix together until it's almost like a paste. Divide into 12 equal portions and roll into balls, then place them on the lined tray. Bake in the preheated oven for 20 minutes, until the balls are golden and crispy at the edges.

Meanwhile, whisk all the sauce ingredients together in a small bowl and serve as a dip alongside the tuna balls.

6 x 92g tins of tuna, drained
½ red onion, peeled and finely diced
2 garlic cloves, peeled and crushed
1 egg, beaten
4 tbsp ground almonds
1 tbsp chilli flakes
1 tsp ground ginger
½ small bunch of fresh coriander, chopped
1 tbsp toasted sesame oil
1 tbsp tamari or soy sauce

FOR THE SAUCE:
juice of ½ lime
1½ tbsp maple syrup or honey
1½ tbsp tahini
1 tbsp rice vinegar
1 tsp tamari or soy sauce
1 tsp hot sauce

Beef parcels

Your protein and greens wrapped up in one – literally!

Preheat the oven to 200°C.

Put the courgettes and asparagus in a medium-sized bowl. Drizzle with the olive oil and season with salt and pepper.

Put the minute steaks on a cutting board and place a small handful of the courgette and asparagus mix in the middle. Roll up each steak around the vegetables and secure them like a parcel with a few toothpicks.

Place the parcels on a baking tray and cook in the preheated oven for 15 minutes, until the steaks are cooked through. Serve with some hummus alongside.

½ small courgette, cut into matchsticks
150g small asparagus tips
1 tbsp olive oil
salt and freshly ground black pepper
4 minute steaks
hummus (page 34), to serve

Lunchbox loves

A little bit of lunchbox inspo for you here for every day of the week! Lunch prep is by far the most challenging, as you want to prep something that isn't going to take ages but will still taste good later. These super salad boxes will make you fall in love with salad again and will give you a nice repertoire of recipes so you never get bored. And if you're wondering where the name came from for the 'same same' lunchbox, it's a phrase that gets used a lot on my sister and me when we go to Thailand on holiday together. I just had to name it that for her, since that lunchbox is her favourite (the Mexican one is my fave!).

```
HOW TO MAKE YOUR LUNCHBOX...

These couldn't be simpler: just toss all the
salad ingredients together before packing in
an airtight container or lunchbox, or you could
arrange the ingredients in separate neat rows
for more of a wow factor. To make the dressings,
whisk everything together in a glass or jar until
smooth. If making the Mexican dressing, blitz all
those ingredients in a blender or NutriBullet.
Put the dressings in a separate small container
and drizzle over the salad when you're ready to
eat. Easy!
```

MEXICAN
ONE

PROTEIN
ONE

VEGGIE
ONE

GREEN ONE

EASY ONE

SAME SAME

1. Green one

2 hardboiled eggs mashed with
   1 tbsp pesto (see page 110
   for how to cook the eggs and
   page 32 for the pesto)

1 small courgette, spiralized

½ ripe avocado, peeled, stoned
   and diced

handful of steamed broccoli
   florets

handful of frozen peas, thawed

2 tbsp pumpkin seeds, toasted

2. Easy one

2 hardboiled eggs (see page
   110 for how to cook the eggs)

½ x 400g tin of chickpeas,
   drained and rinsed

40g cooked bulgur (page 36)

20g feta cheese, cut into small
   cubes

handful of cress

2 tbsp mixed seeds, toasted

3. Protein one

1 x 60g tin of tuna mixed with
   1 tbsp Greek yogurt, ½ tsp Dijon
   mustard and a squeeze of lemon

60g cooked green lentils

40g cooked quinoa (page 39)

handful of baby spinach

1 tbsp whole almonds, toasted

1 tbsp pumpkin seeds, toasted

4. Mexican one

100–120g cooked beef mince

80g roasted sweet potato

4 cherry tomatoes, halved

½ ripe avocado, peeled, stoned
    and sliced

2 handfuls of baby spinach

1 lime, cut into wedges

2 tbsp tinned black beans,
    drained and rinsed

2 tbsp tinned sweetcorn

1 tbsp chopped fresh coriander

FOR THE SAUCE

1 roasted red pepper

2 tbsp nut milk

1 tbsp cashew butter

1 tbsp nutritional yeast

5. Veggie one

½ x 400g tin of chickpeas,
    drained and rinsed

40g cooked quinoa (page 39) or
    brown rice (page 38)

1 cooked beetroot, cut into
    quarters

handful of roasted chopped
    butternut squash

handful of roasted Brussels
    sprouts

1 tbsp mixed roasted nuts

1 tbsp dried fruit, such as goji
    berries, cranberries or diced
    dates

FOR THE DRESSING:

juice of ½ orange

1 tbsp olive oil

1½ tsp honey

1 tsp ground cumin

6. Same same

1 small carrot, peeled and
    spiralized

½ courgette, spiralized

½ red pepper, thinly sliced

1 spring onion, thinly sliced

30g cashews, toasted and
    roughly chopped

20g bean sprouts

1 tbsp chopped fresh coriander

FOR THE DRESSING:

juice of 1 lime

4 tbsp water

1 tbsp tahini

2 tsp tamari or soy sauce

1 tsp maple syrup

1 tsp chilli powder

5.
Snacks

Snappy seeds

I always have nuts and seeds in my press, as they're the perfect nibble and are ideal for adding crunch and texture to salads. However, they are also very easy to overeat – I'm looking at myself here! – so when I prep my nut and seed snacks, I portion them into jars or tubs rather than one large container so that I don't eat them all in one sitting.

Preheat the oven to 200°C.

Put the seeds and tamari in a bowl and stir until all the seeds are coated with the sauce, then tip out onto a baking tray and toast in the preheated oven for 10 minutes, stirring halfway through.

Let the seeds cool, then combine with the dried fruit and cacao nibs. Store in a jar for up to a month.

150g seeds, such as pumpkin, sunflower and/or sesame
1½ tbsp tamari or soy sauce
4 tbsp chopped dried fruit, such as goji berries or pitted dates
2 tbsp cacao nibs

Curry cashews

This comes with a warning: you may lose a few cashews while making these, since they're way too good not to nibble a few! Divide into portions immediately or risk eating the lot.

Preheat the oven to 190°C.

Put the curry powder, oil and honey in a small bowl and whisk together into a paste, then add the nuts and stir until they're all evenly coated. Tip out onto a baking tray and cook in the preheated oven for 15 minutes, until toasted. Let the nuts cool, then store in a jar for up to two weeks.

1 tbsp curry powder

1 tbsp olive oil

1 tsp honey or maple syrup

200g raw cashews

Sweet hummus with sliced fruit

Hummus comes in all shapes and sizes, so don't discount this sweet chickpea number until you've given it a go.

Put all the ingredients except the fruit in a food processor or mini blender and blitz until smooth, with no visible traces of chickpeas. You might need to stop and scrape down the sides of the bowl once or twice and it could take anywhere from 3 to 5 minutes to blend the hummus completely.

Spoon the hummus into a bowl and scatter over some chopped pistachios and cacao nibs if you like. Dip the sliced apples or pears or even celery sticks or carrot batons in the sweet hummus, or spread it on some oat bread. You can store any leftover hummus in an airtight container in the fridge for up to four days.

1 x 400g tin of chickpeas, drained and rinsed

4 tbsp crunchy peanut butter

3 tbsp maple syrup

2 tbsp raw cacao powder

2 tbsp coconut oil, melted

1 tsp vanilla powder

1 tsp ground cinnamon

1 apple and/or pear, cored and sliced

chopped pistachios, to serve (optional)

cacao nibs, to serve (optional)

Mackerel pâté

I love the texture of this omega-rich snack. The pâté is perfect with something crunchy like raw veggie sticks or toasted rye bread.

Put all the ingredients in a food processor or blender (a NutriBullet works well) and blend for 1 to 2 minutes, until smooth but with a few bits of sunflower seeds still visible to give the pâté a nice crunch.

This pâté is perfect served with veggie crudités, rye toast or eggs. You can store any leftovers in a jar in the fridge for up to three days. Or for a snack on the go, spoon some pâté into the bottom of a jar, then stick raw veggies down into the pâté, seal the jar with a lid and throw it into your bag.

2 x 110g tins of mackerel in olive oil, drained
50g sunflower seeds
1 garlic clove, peeled and crushed
2 tbsp chopped fresh flat-leaf parsley
1½ tbsp Greek yogurt (or tahini for a dairy-free option)
1 tbsp lemon juice
½ tbsp apple cider vinegar
½ tbsp Dijon mustard
pinch of sea salt

Egg + almond hero snack

Are you nuts for eggs? Me too! Check out this super-delicious snack featuring my two hero foods.

Put the eggs in a saucepan and add enough cold water to cover them by 2.5cm. Bring to the boil, then remove from the heat, cover the pan and let the eggs sit in the hot water for 12 minutes. Remove the eggs from the water with a slotted spoon and run under cold water to cool them down. When they're cool enough to handle, peel the eggs and cut them in half. To serve, just spread a little almond butter on each halved egg. I know it's weird, but I love it!

2 eggs
1 tbsp almond butter

Parmesan + smoked salmon oat scones

If you follow me on social media, then you know how much I love scones. They really remind me of growing up and were one of the first things I learned how to make, so this is definitely my ultimate savoury snack. But you can sub the ingredients to make these your own – the smoked salmon can be replaced with Parma ham, diced cooked bacon or even sun-dried tomatoes for a vegetarian version.

Preheat the oven to 200°C. Line a baking tray with non-stick baking paper.

Put the oats in a food processor and blitz them into a flour, then tip the oat flour into a large bowl. Add the grated Parmesan, herbs, baking powder and baking soda and stir to combine. Add the beaten egg, yogurt and coconut oil and use your hands to work the mixture into a dough, then work in the smoked salmon pieces.

Tip the dough out onto a cutting board and pat it down until it's 5cm thick. Using a scone cutter, stamp out five scones, put them on the lined tray and sprinkle some extra oats on top, pressing them down lightly to stick.

Bake in the preheated oven for 20 minutes, until the scones are golden around the edges and firm. These are best eaten warm, but they're also good if you let them cool before stashing them in an airtight container or ziplock bag to have as a snack later.

300g porridge oats, plus extra for sprinkling
100g grated Parmesan cheese
1 tbsp dried Italian herbs
¾ tsp baking powder
½ tsp baking soda
1 egg, beaten
5 tbsp natural yogurt
2 tbsp coconut oil, at room temperature
100g smoked salmon, cut into bite-sized pieces

Post-training burger bites

I'm usually frantically jumping straight from the gym to a job, so I need to make sure I'm not skipping meals, especially after a hard workout. These burger bites deliver a nice balance of lean protein and carbs to help your muscles rebuild and recover.

Preheat the oven to 200°C.

Put all the ingredients in a medium-sized bowl and use your hands to combine everything together. Roll into eight balls (it will be a loose mix, but you'll still be able to shape them) and place on a non-stick baking tray. Bake in the preheated oven for 20 minutes, until cooked through.

You can eat these hot out of the oven, but if you're like me and you need to eat them on the go, they're good cold too. Just let them cool fully, then store them in an airtight container in the fridge.

380g turkey breast mince

160g cooked brown or basmati rice (page 38)

1 small carrot, peeled and grated

1 celery stick, finely diced

1 egg, beaten

1 garlic clove, peeled and crushed

1 tbsp tomato purée

1 tbsp dried oregano

salt and freshly ground black pepper

MY LOVE/HATE HIIT SESSION

This is super-high intensity but a serious calorie burner! Do 20 to 30 seconds on each one, moving straight into the next one, then 1 minute of rest — aim to do 8 to 10 rounds.

- Jumping lunges
- Bear crawls
- Mountain climber
- Burpees

The original hun bun

A one-bowl mix giving you a stun hun in minutes. Scale up the recipe for when your huns are over!

Preheat the oven to 180°C.

Put the egg, protein powder and almond butter together in a small bowl and blend with a hand-held electric beater – it should have a caramel-like consistency. Spoon into a silicone cupcake case (or use two paper cases for extra sturdiness if you don't have a silicone one) and put the case on a small baking tray to make it easier to put in the oven.

Bake in the preheated oven for 10 minutes, until the top and edges are firm but the bun is still a little gooey in the middle. Set aside to cool for 2 minutes before tucking in, but be warned that the gooeyness in the centre means it might burst when you take a bite!

1 egg
2 tbsp vanilla or chocolate whey protein powder
1 heaped tbsp almond butter

The only protein bars

Like it says on the tin, this is the only protein bar recipe you will ever need! These are my favourite bars and I love making them. They're dead simple, so there's no way you can mess them up.

Put the almond butter, protein powder, honey and oils in a medium-sized bowl and mix together into a dough, then mix in the almonds and sesame seeds. The dough should be easy to roll with your hands – not too sticky, but also not so dry that it doesn't stick together.

Line a 15cm x 10cm baking tin or a 1lb loaf tin with clingfilm. Tip the dough into the lined tin and press it down firmly in an even layer. Place in the freezer for 10 minutes to harden up a bit before turning out onto a cutting board, peeling off the clingfilm and slicing into five bars.

You can store the bars layered between pieces of parchment paper in an airtight container in the fridge for up to 12 days, but I like to keep mine in the freezer so that when I grab one for on the go, it will be the perfect texture by the time I get to dig in.

100g almond butter

65g protein powder (I use a
    pea/hemp/rice mix)

4 tbsp honey

1 tbsp flaxseed oil or Udo's Oil

1 tbsp olive oil

60g whole almonds, toasted
    and chopped

4 tbsp sesame seeds

Wonder cookies

The best excuse for a cookie! These are crispy on the outside and chewy on the inside. Eat them warm for the most satisfying munch.

Preheat the oven to 180°C.

Put the banana and coconut (yep, that's really all you need!) in a blender or smoothie maker and blitz for 1 minute, until smooth and starting to come together into a ball.

Pinch off a tablespoon of dough and roll it into a ball. Place on a non-stick baking tray and press it down until it's 1cm thick. This is when you can add two or three raisins or chocolate chips (if using) and press them down into the cookie. Repeat with the rest of the dough until you've made six cookies in total.

Bake in the preheated oven for 18 to 20 minutes, until the cookies are golden brown and crispy around the edges. Let the cookies cool on a wire rack for 5 minutes before tucking in. You can store any leftovers in an airtight container in the fridge for up to three days.

1 overripe banana, peeled

100g desiccated coconut

handful of raisins or dark chocolate chips (*optional*)

Oatmeal raisin balls

Just a few of my favourite things, all wrapped up together for a handy energy boost on the go.

Start by melting the coconut oil in a small saucepan set over a low heat. Remove from the heat and let it cool a little, then add the remaining ingredients and mix everything together until well combined. Roll into balls (you should be able to make about 15) and place on a plate in the fridge for 30 minutes to firm up.

You can store the balls in an airtight container in the fridge for up to a week for a quick, no-fuss lunchbox filler.

4 tbsp coconut oil

150g porridge oats

5 tbsp peanut butter

2 tbsp honey

handful of raisins

Courgette sliders

So simple, yet so good. These are the ultimate healthy snack to have with a cuppa or a natter with a mate or for your lunchbox.

Spread a little hummus on a courgette slice, then scatter over a pinch of toasted seeds and dried fruit. Repeat with the remaining ingredients – you should get about six sliders from one small courgette.

2–3 tbsp of your favourite hummus (I love to use the roasted carrot hummus from my *Natural Born Feeder* book or the plain one on page 34)

1 small courgette, cut lengthways into slices 5mm thick

4 tbsp mixed seeds, toasted

1 tbsp dried fruit, such as goji berries

Mini meatloaves, two ways

These are seriously satisfying mouthfuls! They're a really nice combination of a sweet texture and savoury flavour. This is the recipe that people are most surprised by – you won't believe just how tasty they are until you make them yourself.

Preheat the oven to 200°C. Grease a 12-hole muffin tin by rubbing a little olive oil in each cup.

If you're making the turkey meatloaves, put the grated sweet potato in the middle of a clean tea towel, gather up the edges into a ball and give it a good squeeze to get rid of any excess water. For both versions, put all the ingredients in a large bowl and mix together until well combined. Spoon 2 tablespoons of the meatloaf mix into each mould and press down using the back of the spoon.

Bake in the preheated oven for 20 minutes, until the mini meatloaves are cooked through. Let the meatloaves cool in the tin for 5 minutes before turning them out onto a plate.

FOR THE BEEF CAKE:

1 tbsp olive oil

380g beef mince

55g mozzarella or Parmesan cheese, grated

3 eggs, lightly beaten

1 large onion, peeled and finely diced

1 large carrot, peeled and finely diced

2 garlic cloves, peeled and crushed

2 sprigs of fresh rosemary, needles stripped and finely chopped

4 tbsp ground almonds

1 tbsp dried parsley

salt and freshly ground black pepper

FOR THE TASTY TURKEY:

1 tbsp olive oil

380g turkey mince

3 eggs, lightly beaten

1 small sweet potato, peeled and grated

1 red onion, peeled and finely diced

2 handfuls of mixed seeds

handful of dried cranberries

4 tbsp ground almonds

2 tbsp dried thyme

1 tbsp desiccated coconut

salt and freshly ground black pepper

Wilko snax

The main man in my life, my adopted puppy, Wilko, deserves his very own recipe! Wilko takes no commands and he chews all my shoes – even my passport once – but he gives the best cuddles. These biscuits won't make your dog smell, if you get me. All you dog owners know what I'm talking about!

Preheat the oven to 180°C. Line a baking tray with non-stick baking paper.

Put the oats in a food processor and blitz them into a flour, then tip the oat flour into a medium-sized bowl. Add the beaten egg, chicken stock and peanut butter and mix until combined into a sticky dough, then mix in the sweet potato and bacon pieces.

Dust a cutting board with a little extra oat flour. Pinch off a piece of dough about the size of a golf ball, then use your hands to roll it into a cylinder about 5cm long and 2cm thick. Make two round ball shapes at one end (yep, it looks like a willy, I know!) and make another two ball shapes at the other end, and there you have it – it should look like a bone.

Place the biscuits on the lined tray and bake in the preheated oven for 20 minutes, until firm and golden brown. Let the biscuits cool completely on a wire rack, then store them in an airtight container for up to three weeks.

200g porridge oats, plus extra oat flour for dusting
1 egg, beaten
½ chicken stock cube dissolved in 100ml hot water
2 tbsp smooth peanut butter
2 handfuls of peeled and grated sweet potato
2 cooked bacon or turkey rashers, fat trimmed off and chopped into tiny pieces

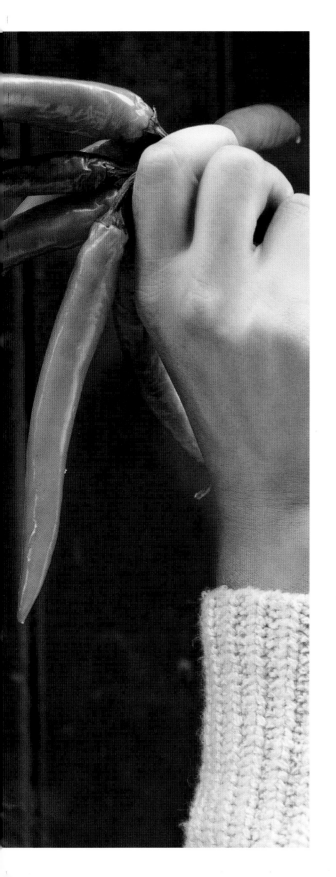

6.
Dinner

Chicken Tray bake with squash + pesto

Move over, one-pot wonders – tray bakes are here! This and the one on page 158 are two of my favourites, but change them up to use whatever you have in your fridge or opt for turkey, fish or lamb.

Preheat the oven to 210°C.

Put the pesto, olive oil, lemon zest and juice and some salt and pepper in a large bowl and whisk together. Add the chicken and veg and stir to coat in the pesto mixture.

Tip everything out onto a large baking tray or roasting tin and cook in the preheated oven for 20 minutes, until the chicken is cooked through and the veg are tender.

6 tbsp pesto (page 32)

2 tbsp olive oil

zest and juice of 1 lemon

salt and freshly ground black pepper

6 chicken legs or thighs (or a mix of both), skin on and bone in

2 large red onions, peeled and sliced into rings

1 small butternut squash, peeled and thinly sliced into rings, then cut again into quarters

Piri piri chicken tray bake

Tray bakes couldn't be easier – just throw everything onto a baking tray and pop it in the oven. If I'm prepping these ahead of time, I put all the ingredients in a ziplock bag so that I can just tip it out onto the tray as soon as I walk in the door.

Preheat the oven to 210°C.

Put the olive oil, oregano, paprika, honey, vinegar and some salt and pepper in a large bowl and whisk together. Add the chicken, peppers, corn, sprouts (if using), chillies and garlic and stir to coat the chicken and veg in the spicy oil.

Tip everything out onto a large baking tray or roasting tin and cook in the preheated oven for 20 minutes, until the chicken is cooked through and the veg are tender.

2 tbsp olive oil

1 tbsp dried oregano

1 tbsp paprika

1 tbsp honey

1 tsp apple cider vinegar

salt and freshly ground black pepper

6 chicken legs or thighs (or a mix
   of both), skin on and bone in

3 red peppers, sliced

2 corn on the cob, each one cut
   into thirds

200g Brussels sprouts, halved
   (*optional*)

6–7 bird's eye chillies,
   deseeded and finely chopped

3 large garlic cloves, peeled and
   halved

ASAP chicken, two ways

I'm always looking for ways to tart up an auld chicken breast. Consistency is key when you're trying to lead a healthy lifestyle, so having some variations of your basics up your sleeve is a must. This recipe serves one, so just scale it up if you have more people to feed.

Preheat the oven to 200°C. Line a baking tray with non-stick baking paper.

For either filling, just mix all the ingredients together in a small bowl.

Cut the chicken fillet in half horizontally so that it opens out like a book, making sure you don't cut it all the way through. Spread the filling in the centre, then roll up the fillet tightly to enclose the filling.

Place on the lined tray, seam side down, and cook in the preheated oven for 25 minutes, until the chicken is completely cooked through.

1 chicken fillet

FOR THE CURRY FILLING:

1 tbsp nut butter

1 tbsp tamari or soy sauce

1 tsp curry powder

1 tsp honey

1 lime, sliced

FOR THE GARLIC +
HERB FILLING:

1 garlic clove, peeled and crushed

2 tbsp ground almonds

1 tbsp dried Italian herbs

1 tbsp olive oil

salt and freshly ground black pepper

Chicken satay skewers

This recipe is one of my meal prep heroes. The satay sauce gets super crispy under the grill and makes the chicken into a special occasion meal, because let's be honest, chicken can be pretty boring.

Preheat the grill to high. Line a baking tray with tin foil.

Put all the ingredients except the chicken in a bowl and whisk together to form a paste. Working with one strip of chicken at a time, rub them in the paste until they're each covered in a thin layer.

Thread the chicken strips onto three metals skewers and place on the lined baking tray. Pop the tray under the grill and cook for 16 to 18 minutes, turning the skewers over halfway through, until the chicken is completely cooked. For the last 5 minutes of the cooking time, drizzle the chicken with any leftover satay sauce.

These skewers taste great hot or cold, so you could either have these right away for your dinner or let them cool down before placing in an airtight container for your lunch the next day. They send off an inviting aroma when you open your lunchbox, so be prepared for everyone to ask you what you're having!

2 tbsp almond butter

1½ tbsp sesame oil

1 tbsp tamari or soy sauce

1 tbsp desiccated coconut

1½ tsp honey or maple syrup (optional)

1 tsp curry powder

1 tsp cayenne pepper

2 chicken fillets, cut into thin strips

Pronto pad thai

I was never fully sold on pad thai until I travelled to Thailand, but once I had it there it became one of my favourite dishes. Unfortunately I can't have the original every day, so I created this healthy version to 'tuk-tuk' into.

Whisk together all the ingredients for the sauce in a small bowl. Set aside.

Steam the spiralized sweet potato for 6 to 8 minutes, until the 'noodles' are slightly tender but still holding their shape.

While that's steaming, put a wok over a high heat. Once it's smoking hot, add the oil and swirl it around until it has melted, then add the chicken strips and fry, stirring constantly, for 4 to 5 minutes. Add the prawns, pepper, spring onion and garlic and cook for 3 to 4 minutes.

Toss in the bean sprouts and the steamed sweet potato 'noodles' and give them a quick stir. Create a well in the centre of the pan, crack in the egg and scramble it with a spoon. Once the egg is cooked, stir in the sauce and remove the wok from the heat.

Transfer the pad thai to two bowls and serve with the peanuts and spring onion scattered on top and two lime wedges on the side.

1 large sweet potato (300g), peeled and spiralized
1 tbsp coconut oil
2 chicken fillets, sliced into thin strips
4–6 large prawns
½ red pepper, thinly sliced
1 spring onion, chopped
1 garlic clove, peeled and crushed
100g bean sprouts
1 egg

FOR THE SAUCE:
2.5cm piece of fresh ginger, peeled and grated
juice of 1 lime
2 tbsp tamari or soy sauce
2 tbsp water
1 tbsp honey
1 tbsp sesame oil
1 tsp rice vinegar

TO SERVE:
25g peanuts, crushed
1 spring onion, thinly sliced on the diagonal
1 lime, cut into wedges

Chicken, sweet potato + peanut curry

This recipe is a marriage of two great things: curry and peanut butter. Don't leave out the wholegrain mustard – I know it sounds a little odd, but it really makes this dish. This was the winning dinner when we shot the photos for the book, so it's a real crowd pleaser.

Heat the olive oil in a large, deep pot set over a high heat. Add the onion and cook for 2 to 3 minutes, until golden brown and beginning to crisp. Toss in the chicken and cook for 5 to 6 minutes, stirring regularly, until the chicken is white on the outside. Add the sweet potato cubes, garlic, ginger, spices and some salt and pepper and cook for 2 minutes, then pour in the stock.

Cover the pot with a lid and bring to the boil, then reduce the heat and simmer for 15 minutes. Add the peanut butter, mustard and tomato purée and stir for about 1 minute, until evenly combined.

Ladle the curry into bowls and serve with fresh coriander leaves, sliced banana and a dollop of Greek yogurt on top and cooked basmati rice on the side.

1 tbsp olive oil

1 large onion, peeled and finely diced

4 chicken fillets, diced

2 large sweet potatoes, peeled and cut into 1.5cm cubes

2 garlic cloves, peeled and crushed

4cm piece of fresh ginger, peeled and grated

1 tbsp ground cumin

1 tbsp ground coriander

1½ tsp chilli powder

1 tsp ground turmeric

salt and freshly ground black pepper

400ml chicken stock

2 heaped tbsp crunchy or smooth peanut butter

2 tbsp wholegrain mustard

1 tbsp tomato purée

TO SERVE:
fresh coriander leaves
1 ripe banana, peeled and sliced
Greek yogurt
cooked basmati rice (page 38)

Teriyaki chicken zoodles

I love getting a good bang for my buck with my meals, and this is definitely one of those. The zoodles bulk out the dish, leaving you nicely full while also getting tons of greens in. It's the perfect everyday fake-away.

Whisk all the sauce ingredients together in a small bowl and set aside.

Heat the olive oil in a wok or a large pan set over a high heat. Once the oil is sizzling, add the chicken strips and cook for 7 minutes, until they're white on the outside with some browned edges.

Toss in the carrot and broccoli and cook, stirring regularly, for 6 minutes, until the veg are slightly tender but still have a bit of crunch. Add the courgettes and stir to work the 'zoodles' towards the base of the pan. Cook for 2 minutes to heat them through. Add the garlic and cook for 1 minute, just until it's fragrant.

Pour in the sauce and stir for a moment before dividing everything between two bowls. Scatter over some extra sesame seeds and serve with lime wedges on the side.

1 tbsp olive oil

2 chicken fillets, cut into strips

1 large carrot, peeled and thinly sliced on the diagonal

250g broccoli florets

2 large courgettes, spiralized

2 garlic cloves, peeled and crushed

1 lime, cut into wedges, to serve

FOR THE TERIYAKI SAUCE:

2.5cm piece of fresh ginger, peeled and finely diced

2 tbsp sesame seeds, plus extra to garnish

1 tbsp tamari or soy sauce

1 tbsp rice vinegar

2 tsp honey

Beef + cauli shepherd's pie skillet

There is something just so comforting and nostalgic about shepherd's pie. It's particularly nice to have a healthy, hearty dish like this when the cold evenings start to settle in. You only use egg yolks in the mash, so save the whites and make the skinny crêpes on page 70 for breakfast.

Preheat the oven to 200°C or the grill to high.

Start by steaming the cauliflower for about 10 minutes, until the florets are tender. Pat them dry to remove any excess water, then place in a blender with the egg yolks and some salt and pepper. Blitz to a smooth, creamy purée and set aside.

While the cauliflower is steaming, heat the olive oil in a large ovenproof frying pan set over a medium heat. Add the chopped onion and cook for 2 to 3 minutes, until lightly browned, then add the garlic and cook for 1 minute, just until it's fragrant. Add the mince and cook, stirring, for 8 to 10 minutes, until completely browned. Stir in the carrot, celery, mushrooms and thyme leaves and cook for 2 minutes, then add the frozen peas, stock, tamari, tomato purée and allspice and remove the pan from the heat. Spoon the cauli mash over the mince and spread it out evenly to cover the top, then scatter over the grated cheese (if using).

Place the pan in the preheated oven or under the grill and cook for 8 minutes, until the mash is starting to turn golden and crispy. Garnish with one or two small thyme sprigs, bring the pan straight to the table (but keep the handle covered with a towel or pot holder, as it will still be hot!) and let everyone help themselves.

1 tbsp olive oil

½ large onion, peeled and finely diced

2 large garlic cloves, peeled and crushed

600g lean beef mince

1 carrot, peeled and diced

2 celery stalks, diced

100g button mushrooms, wiped clean and finely diced

1 tbsp fresh thyme leaves, plus extra sprigs to garnish

2 handfuls of frozen peas

100ml beef or chicken stock

1 tbsp tamari or soy sauce

1 tbsp tomato purée

¼ tsp ground allspice

FOR THE CAULI MASH:

2 heads of cauliflower, broken into florets

2 egg yolks

salt and freshly ground black pepper

50g mozzarella or Parmesan cheese, grated (optional)

Red curry burgers

Whether you're having a barbecue or making these as part of your meal prep, these simple, no-fuss burgers taste deadly.

Preheat the oven to 200°C. Line a baking tray with non-stick baking paper.

Put the mince, egg, onion, curry paste and some salt and pepper in a medium-sized bowl. Use your hands to get stuck in and mix it all together, then form into eight small burgers and place them on the lined tray.

Cook in the preheated oven for 20 minutes, turning the burgers over halfway through to make sure they cook thoroughly. If you want to cook them even faster, you can pan-fry the burgers. Small burgers will cook in roughly 10 minutes (5 minutes on each side).

While the burgers are cooking, whisk together all the sauce ingredients in a small bowl and serve with the burgers.

600g lean beef mince

1 egg, beaten

½ large red onion, peeled and finely diced or grated

2 tbsp red curry paste (buy a good-quality brand with no added sugar)

salt and freshly ground black pepper

FOR THE SAUCE:

juice of 1 small lemon or lime

4 tbsp Greek or coconut yogurt

1 tbsp dried parsley

1 tsp dried Italian herbs

Asian-style beef koftas with creamy cashew dip

These are the perfect small bite for friends popping around. They're a twist on typical koftas, packed full of flavour and with an added kick from the hot sauce. These can also be made into meatballs or burgers and are delicious served with cauli rice or brown rice and of course the dip! Or if you're having a barbecue, throw these on the hot grill and cook the skewers for 3 to 4 minutes on each side.

Preheat the oven to 200°C. Line a baking tray with tin foil.

Put all the ingredients except the mince in a food processor and pulse into a paste. Put the beef mince and the paste in a large bowl and use your hands to mix it all together, then form the beef into oval kofta shapes (you should aim to make 12). Thread three koftas onto a metal skewer, making four skewers in total.

Place the skewers on the lined baking tray and cook in the preheated oven for 15 minutes. Turn the skewers over and cook for 5 minutes more, until the beef is nicely browned and cooked through.

Meanwhile, to make the cashew dip, grind the nuts to a flour-like consistency in a food processor or blender (a NutriBullet works well). Pour the coconut milk into a small saucepan set over a medium heat and let it come up to a simmer, then add the ground cashews and cook, stirring constantly, for 5 to 6 minutes, until the sauce is thick and creamy. Squeeze in the lime juice and stir to combine, then remove from the heat.

Serve the koftas with small bowls of the dipping sauce on the side.

1 shallot, peeled and chopped

2 lemongrass stalks, white part only, roughly chopped

2 garlic cloves, peeled and chopped

2.5cm piece of fresh ginger, peeled and chopped

½ bunch of coriander, leaves picked

1½ tbsp tamari, soy sauce or coconut aminos

1 tbsp hot sauce or sriracha sauce

1 tbsp honey (optional)

600g lean beef mince

FOR THE CREAMY CASHEW DIP:

60g raw cashews

200ml full-fat coconut milk

juice of 1 lime

Beef + ginger stir-fry

I know a stir-fry sounds a little boring, but this is actually one of my favourite meals, flavour-wise. It hits all the right spots: it's sweet, salty, tangy, chewy and has a bit of bite. It serves one because it's the dish I always make on a night in when I have the house to myself – face mask on, Netflix on, a bowl of this and some Wilko time!

Heat the olive oil in a wok or a large frying pan set over a high heat. Once the oil is smoking hot, add the steak strips and cook for 2 to 3 minutes to sear them off. Add the carrot, sesame seeds and ginger and cook for 1 minute more to toast the seeds, then stir in the cooked rice or quinoa.

Whisk the sesame oil, tamari and honey together in a glass or jar, then pour into the pan and give it a stir to coat the steak and vegetables with the sauce.

Plate up and scatter over the spring onion and fresh coriander.

1 tbsp olive oil

1 lean beef steak, thinly sliced into strips

1 carrot, peeled and grated

20g sesame seeds, toasted

1.25cm piece of fresh ginger, peeled and grated

45g cooked black or wild rice (page 38) or quinoa (page 39)

1 spring onion, sliced, to serve

handful of fresh coriander, chopped, to serve

FOR THE SAUCE:

1 tbsp sesame oil

1 tbsp tamari or soy sauce

1 tbsp honey

Burrito bowl

You really can't go wrong with a burrito, and this burrito bowl is a savage meal prep dish or one to make in bulk. You can change it to suit your tastes by using minced beef, turkey or even cooked lentils (page 39). I usually have this with cauliflower rice, but you could use cooked brown rice (page 38) too.

Heat the oil in a large frying pan set over a high heat. Once the oil starts sizzling, toss in the onion and cook for 2 minutes, stirring, until browned and softened. Add most of the chillies (keep some back for garnish) and the garlic and cook for 1 minute more, just until the garlic is fragrant. Add the mince or lentils and cook for 5 to 6 minutes, until the meat is browned and almost cooked through. Use a wooden spoon to break up the mince as it cooks.

Add the peppers, spices and some salt and pepper, give it a good stir and continue to cook on a high heat for 3 to 4 minutes, stirring now and again to ensure everything cooks evenly. The peppers should still have a little crunch, which is why they're not added sooner.

Now stir in the black beans, sweetcorn, cauliflower rice, tomato purée and honey (if using – it adds a nice bit of sweetness with the spice) and cook for 2 to 3 minutes, until the beans, corn and cauli rice are warmed through. Or you could keep the cauli rice separate and use it as a base in the bottom of the bowl, then pile the rest of the ingredients on top.

Divide between four bowls and serve with some avocado slices and lime wedges on the side and a dollop of Greek yogurt on top, then scatter over a few of the reserved chillies and some fresh coriander leaves. This is also an awesome lunchbox for the next day.

2 tbsp olive oil

1 small onion, peeled and finely diced

2 fresh red chillies, deseeded and thinly sliced or finely chopped

2 garlic cloves, peeled and finely chopped

500g lean beef or turkey mince

1 red pepper, cut into cubes

½ yellow pepper, cut into cubes

½ green pepper, cut into cubes

1 tbsp ground cumin

2 tsp ground coriander

1 tsp smoked paprika

salt and freshly ground black pepper

1 x 400g tin of black beans, drained and rinsed

1 x 200g tin of sweetcorn

2 small heads of cauliflower, riced (see page 39)

2 tbsp tomato purée

1 tbsp honey (*optional*)

TO SERVE:

1 ripe avocado, peeled, stoned and sliced

limes wedges

Greek yogurt

fresh coriander leaves

Tick-tock Tagine

I just had to make a fast tagine, as it's been my signature dish from the start. This one is so fast and simple that it has completely replaced my original tagine and it's pretty much the only one I make now.

Heat the oil in a large pot set over a high heat. Add the onion and cook for 2 to 3 minutes, stirring to brown it evenly. Add the garlic and ginger and cook for 1 minute, just until the garlic is fragrant, then add the lamb mince and cook for 4 to 5 minutes, until browned all over.

Toss in the squash, dried fruit (if using), spices and some salt and pepper and cook for 2 minutes. Pour in the chopped tomatoes, stock and tomato purée, cover the pot with a lid and simmer for 10 minutes, until the squash is tender. Stir in the chickpeas and cook for 1 minute more to heat them through.

Ladle the tagine into four bowls and garnish with the fresh herbs.

1 tbsp olive oil

1 small red onion, peeled and finely diced

2 garlic cloves, peeled and crushed

2.5cm piece of fresh ginger, peeled and grated

600g lamb mince

½ butternut squash, peeled and diced into 2cm cubes

handful of dried apricots or pitted dates, chopped (*optional*)

1 tbsp ground cumin

1½ tsp paprika

1 tsp ground coriander

1 tsp ground turmeric

1 tsp ground cinnamon

salt and freshly ground black pepper

1 x 400g tin of chopped tomatoes

200ml chicken stock

1 tbsp tomato purée

1 x 400g tin of chickpeas, drained and rinsed

handful of fresh parsley, chopped, to garnish

handful of fresh coriander, chopped, to garnish

Sweet chilli salmon balls with peanut slaw

I think you can see where things are going here – I eat a lot of fish, so it's really important for me to keep things interesting by packing it full of flavour but without adding extra time. Burgers are such a handy meal prep recipe, and if you're like me and you love salmon, they're also a good way to avoid getting bored with it.

Preheat the oven to 200°C. Line a baking tray with tin foil.

Put the salmon, beaten egg, ground almonds, honey and chilli paste in a medium-sized bowl and use a fork to mix everything together. Chill in the fridge while you prep the slaw.

To make the peanut slaw, put the cabbage and carrots in a large bowl and mix together. In a separate small bowl, whisk the lemon juice, peanut butter, tamari and vinegar together. Pour this over the cabbage and carrots and toss until evenly combined, then add the toasted sesame seeds and toss again.

Divide the fish mixture into eight portions and roll into balls. Place on the lined baking tray and bake in the preheated oven for 15 minutes, until golden and crispy around the edges. Serve hot with the peanut slaw on the side.

4 x 62g tins of no-drain salmon
1 egg, beaten
4 tbsp ground almonds
1 tbsp honey
1 tbsp chilli paste

FOR THE PEANUT SLAW:
¼ head of red cabbage, grated
    or finely shredded
¼ head of white cabbage,
    grated or finely shredded
2 small carrots, peeled and grated
juice of 1 lemon
2 tbsp crunchy peanut butter
1 tbsp tamari or soy sauce
1 tbsp rice vinegar
2 tbsp toasted sesame seeds

Poke bowl

I've been slightly obsessed with poke bowls ever since I discovered them on a trip abroad. Thankfully they've become mainstream lately and lots of restaurants have them on the menu, but they're so easy to make at home. Don't fear the raw fish!

Put all the dressing ingredients in a medium-sized bowl and whisk to combine. Add the diced raw fish and stir until it's all completely covered in the dressing. Let this sit while you prep your extras.

Load up your grains or noodles in one half of the bowl, then add the fish in the other half. Top with the sliced avocado, one or two lime wedges, some kimchi and pickled ginger and finish with a few fresh coriander leaves.

2 sushi-grade skinless salmon
   or tuna fillets, diced into cubes

FOR THE DRESSING:
2 tbsp black or white sesame
   seeds, toasted
2 tbsp sesame oil
2 tbsp tamari or soy sauce
1 tbsp rice vinegar or apple cider
   vinegar
1 tbsp honey
½ tsp chilli paste or flakes

TO SERVE:
cooked basmati rice (page 38),
   noodles or quinoa (page 39)
1 ripe avocado, peeled, stoned
   and thinly sliced
1 lime, cut into wedges
kimchi
pickled ginger
fresh coriander leaves

Fish curry in a hurry

I'm not hating on white fish or anything, but it does need a little help in the flavour department, especially if you're like me and you eat it a lot. This creamy, spicy sauce and the quick-fix mash are the perfect partners for your fish.

Melt the coconut oil in a large frying pan set over a medium heat. Add the red peppers and cook for 5 to 8 minutes, stirring now and then, until soft (this will depend on how finely you diced them!). Add the garlic, garam masala and some salt and pepper and stir for 1 minute, then remove from the heat and scrape the peppers into a blender. Add the coconut milk and almond butter and blend into a smooth paste. Set aside.

To make the butter bean mash, pulse the beans in a food processor until smooth. Heat the olive oil in a large pot set over a medium heat, then add the spinach and let it wilt down. Stir in the puréed beans and cook for 2 or 3 minutes to warm them through. Season with a pinch of salt and pepper.

Using the same frying pan that you cooked the peppers in, heat the olive oil over a high heat. Once the oil is sizzling, add the hake pieces and cook for 4 minutes on each side, until golden, crispy and cooked through. Turn the heat down to low, pour in the almond curry sauce and let it simmer for 2 to 3 minutes.

Ladle the curry into four bowls, garnish with fresh coriander leaves and serve the butter bean mash in a separate bowl on the side.

1 tbsp coconut oil

2 red peppers, finely diced

1 garlic clove, peeled and crushed

2 tbsp garam masala or curry powder

salt and freshly ground black pepper

½ x 400ml tin of full-fat coconut milk

2 tbsp almond butter

1 tbsp olive oil

1 x 800g skinless hake fillet, cut into 5cm chunks

fresh coriander leaves, to garnish

FOR THE BUTTER BEAN MASH:

2 x 400g tins of butter beans, drained and rinsed

2 tbsp olive oil

100g baby spinach

Hake + bean bake

Crispy hake on a bed of beans bursting with flavour, all in one pan – it's easy and it saves on the washing-up. What more could you ask for?

Preheat the oven to 200°C.

Pat the hake fillets dry with a piece of kitchen paper. Put the ground almonds, pepper and a pinch of salt on a plate and stir to combine. Put the fish fillets in the almond mix, skin side up, and press down firmly to coat the top of each fillet with the ground almond mix.

Heat the olive oil in a large ovenproof frying pan set over a high heat. Add the fillets to the hot oil, coated side down, and cook for 2 to 3 minutes, until golden, before flipping over and cooking the other side for a further 5 minutes. Remove the fish from the pan and set aside on a plate.

Reduce the heat to medium. Add the beans and tomatoes to the pan, then stir in the pesto and cook for 2 minutes. Place the hake back on top and transfer the pan to the preheated oven. Bake for 12 minutes, until the fish is completely cooked through and the beans are bubbling.

Divide between two wide, shallow bowls and garnish with the fresh basil.

2 hake fillets or any other white fish, skin on

2–3 tbsp ground almonds

1 tbsp ground black pepper

pinch of salt

1 tbsp olive oil

1 x 400g tin of mixed beans, drained and rinsed

1 x 400g tin of chopped tomatoes

1½ tbsp pesto (page 32)

fresh basil leaves, to garnish

Crispy sweet + sour cod

Who else was a fan of a sweet and sour combo takeaway? I was and so was my dad, who only let us get one when my mum was away (sorry for throwing you in the deep end there, John!). I love to recreate my childhood cravings, so here's a healthy, hearty replacement for the takeaways of the past.

Pat the cod dry with a piece of kitchen paper. Put the ground almonds in a medium-sized bowl and add the cod, tossing to lightly coat each piece.

Heat 1 tablespoon of the oil in a non-stick frying pan set over a high heat. Add the cod and fry for 3 to 4 minutes on each side, until golden, crispy and cooked through. Remove the cod from the pan and set aside on a plate.

Put the remaining tablespoon of oil in the same pan, still set over a high heat, then add the onion, carrot and peppers. Cook for 6 minutes, stirring, until softened. Add the garlic, ginger and chilli powder and cook for 1 minute, then add the tomatoes and break them down with the back of the spoon. Bring to the boil, then turn the heat down to medium and simmer for 5 minutes, stirring two or three times, until the sauce has thickened a little.

Add the tamari, honey and vinegar and stir to combine, then add the cod back to the pan and cook for 1 minute more until it's heated through again.

Divide between four wide, shallow bowls and serve with cooked wild rice. Garnish with a few fresh coriander leaves and pop a lime wedge on the side.

1 x 800g skinless cod fillet, cut into 5cm x 2.5cm pieces
8 tbsp ground almonds
2 tbsp olive or coconut oil
1 onion, peeled, halved and thinly sliced
1 large carrot, peeled and thinly sliced
½ red pepper, thinly sliced lengthways
½ yellow pepper, thinly sliced lengthways
1 garlic clove, peeled and crushed
5cm piece of fresh ginger, peeled and grated
1 tbsp chilli powder
1 x 400g tin of whole plum tomatoes
1 tbsp tamari or soy sauce
1 tbsp honey
1 tsp apple cider vinegar
cooked wild rice (page 38), to serve
fresh coriander leaves, to garnish
1–2 limes, halved or cut into wedges, to serve

Red lentil curry pie

A seriously warming, comforting dinner, this is a great meal prep option too. You can try it with different toppings, like sweet potato mash or an oat crust, which is one of my favourite variations.

Preheat the oven to 200°C.

Start by steaming the cauliflower for about 10 minutes, until tender. Pat the florets dry with kitchen paper to absorb any excess water, then place in a high-speed blender. Add a pinch of salt and pepper and blitz to a smooth, creamy purée.

Heat the olive oil in a large ovenproof pan set over a high heat. Add the onion, carrots and garlic and cook for 2 to 3 minutes, until softened. Add the lentils, tomatoes, peas, curry powder and some salt and pepper and simmer for 5 minutes. Remove from the heat and stir in the coconut milk and turmeric, then pour into a large baking dish.

Top with the cauliflower mash and spread it out to cover the filling in an even layer. Sprinkle the mash with the nuts or oats and cook in the preheated oven for 10 minutes, until the mash is golden brown. Or you can skip this step and serve the lentils in a bowl with a dollop of the cauli mash on top.

1 tbsp olive oil

1 onion, peeled and finely diced

2 carrots, peeled and cut into 5mm chunks

2 garlic cloves, peeled and crushed

800g cooked split red lentils (450g uncooked – see page 39)

2 x 400g tins of chopped tomatoes

120g frozen peas

3 tbsp curry powder

salt and freshly ground black pepper

1 x 400ml tin of full-fat coconut milk

1 tsp ground turmeric

FOR THE TOPPING:

2 small heads of cauliflower, broken into florets

4 tbsp ground almonds, cashews or oats

Tacos, three ways

I'm starting to like lettuce tacos more than the regular ones – I'm not kidding! It's the fresh crunch that does it for me. The other great thing about lettuce tacos is that you can really concentrate on your toppings. It's also a great dinner to make for friends coming over, as you can have your fish, meat or veggie options.

To make the fish tacos, first make the yogurt sauce by putting the yogurt, lemon juice and Italian herbs in a small bowl and whisking until well combined. Put the ground almonds and spices in a medium-sized bowl and stir together. Pat the fish dry with a piece of kitchen paper, then add to the bowl and toss until all the pieces are coated. Heat the olive oil in a large frying pan set over a high heat, add the cod and cook for 2 to 3 minutes on each side, until the edges are crispy. Divide the fish between the lettuce cups and top with some shredded iceberg lettuce, chillies and a drizzle of the yogurt sauce.

To make the beef tacos, heat a dry, heavy-based chargrill pan or skillet over a high heat. Brush both sides of the steaks with the oil and season generously with salt and pepper. When the pan is good and hot, add the steaks and cook for 3 minutes on each side. Transfer the steaks to a cutting board and let them rest for 5 minutes before slicing thinly into strips. Divide the steak between the lettuce cups, top with the avocado and cabbage and drizzle with some pesto.

FOR THE FISH TACOS:

4 tbsp Greek yogurt

juice of ½ lemon

1 tbsp dried Italian herbs

1 tbsp ground almonds

1 tbsp chilli powder

1½ tsp paprika

1 tsp ground cumin

250–300g skinless white fish, cut
    into 3cm pieces

1 tbsp olive oil

4 romaine lettuce leaves

handful of iceberg lettuce,
    shredded

1 fresh red chilli, deseeded and
    thinly sliced

FOR THE BEEF TACOS:

2 small sirloin steaks

1 tbsp olive oil

salt and freshly ground black pepper

4 romaine lettuce leaves

1 ripe avocado, peeled, stoned
    and diced

handful of grated red cabbage

2 tbsp pesto (page 32)

To make the cauli tacos, preheat the oven to 200°C and line a baking tray with non-stick baking paper. Break the cauliflower into florets and slice each one into 1cm-thick 'steaks' from top to bottom. Put the oil, maple syrup, paprika, tomato purée, cayenne, cumin, chilli powder and turmeric in a small bowl and whisk together, then rub this on each side of the cauliflower 'steaks'. Put the steaks on the lined tray and roast in the preheated oven for 20 minutes, until crispy and golden. Meanwhile, to make the avocado cream, put the avocado, lemon juice and almond milk in a blender (a NutriBullet works well here) and blitz until smooth. Put one or two steaks into each lettuce cup and top with black beans, sweetcorn, red pepper and avocado cream.

FOR THE ROAST
CAULI TACOS:

1 small head of cauliflower

2 tbsp olive oil

1 tbsp maple syrup or honey

1 tbsp smoked paprika

1 tbsp tomato purée

1½ tsp cayenne pepper

1 tsp ground cumin

1 tsp chilli powder

½ tsp ground turmeric

1 ripe avocado, peeled and stoned

juice of ½ lemon

6 tbsp unsweetened almond milk

6 romaine lettuce leaves

½ x 400g tin of black beans,
    drained and rinsed

1 small tin of sweetcorn

1 red pepper, thinly sliced

Mini oat pizzas

You can't pass up this recipe – just look at that photo! And these pizzas do taste as good as they look. You'll never order a takeaway pizza again once you see how easy these are to make. This recipe makes one mini pizza base, so scale it up depending on how hungry you are.

Preheat the oven to 200°C. Grease a baking tray with olive oil.

In a small bowl combine the oat flour, oregano, yogurt and apple cider vinegar, then stir in 1 tablespoon of the water to make a dough. If the dough is too dry, add the extra tablespoon of water. You should have a slightly wet dough that's easy enough to pick up and roll into a ball without it sticking to your hands. If it is sticking, though, don't worry – just add a tiny bit of extra oat flour.

Roll the dough into a ball and place on the greased tray. Press it down evenly until it's really thin – aim for it to be about 2.5mm thick. Bake in the preheated oven for 10 minutes, until crispy and firm.

Remove the base from the oven and flip it over. Add the sauce to the centre of the base and spread it out with the back of a spoon, leaving a small border clear around the edges, then scatter over your favourite toppings. Return the pizza to the oven and bake for 5 or 6 minutes more, until your toppings are heated through.

FOR THE BASE:

olive oil, for greasing

2 tbsp oat flour

1 tsp dried oregano

1 tsp natural, Greek or soya yogurt

½ tsp apple cider vinegar

1–2 tbsp water

SAUCE OPTIONS:

tomato sauce

puréed red peppers

pesto (page 32)

hummus (don't cook it though!)
(page 34)

TOPPING IDEAS:

- cooked shredded chicken
- cooked turkey mince
- dry-cured chorizo
- cooked diced bacon
- chopped sun-dried tomatoes
- thinly sliced cherry tomatoes

- thinly sliced mushrooms
- halved or thinly sliced olives
- thinly sliced spring onions
- thinly sliced radishes
- thinly sliced or shredded Brussels sprouts

- cubes of roasted butternut squash
- diced ripe avocado (don't cook)
- shredded cabbage
- sweetcorn
- fresh peas
- crumbled feta cheese
- goat's cheese
- fresh herbs

The tastiest veggie stew

I try to have veggie-based meals at least three nights a week, and I probably make this one the most, as it's pretty handy for meal prep and it gets better as it ages – like yourself!

First prep the tomatoes. Dice two tomatoes into 2.5cm chunks and set aside. Place the other three tomatoes in a food processor or blender (a NutriBullet works well) and blitz until smooth (it may turn a pink colour, but don't worry, that's okay).

Melt the coconut oil in a large pot set over a medium heat. Add the onions and give them a quick stir, then cover the pot with a lid and sweat for 5 minutes, until softened. Stir in the squash and celery and cook for 4 minutes. Add the garlic, cumin and some salt and pepper and cook for 1 minute more, just until the garlic is fragrant.

Pour in the stock, then add the diced tomatoes, courgette and tomato purée. Turn the heat up and boil for 4 or 5 minutes before turning the heat down to low, covering the pot with a lid and simmering the stew for 15 minutes. Add the peas for the final 2 minutes of the cooking time and leave the pot uncovered.

Stir in the parsley and serve in bowls with some cooked quinoa. You can store any leftovers in an airtight container in the fridge for up to three days.

5 large vine-ripened tomatoes

1 tbsp coconut oil

2 red onions, peeled and finely chopped

1 large butternut squash, peeled and diced into 2cm pieces

2 large celery sticks, sliced

2 garlic cloves, peeled and finely diced

1 tbsp ground cumin

salt and freshly ground black pepper

500ml low-sodium vegetable stock

1 courgette, quartered and sliced

1 tbsp tomato purée

150g frozen peas

1 small bunch of fresh flat-leaf parsley, chopped

cooked quinoa (page 39), to serve

Peanut, squash + chickpea curry

You can blitz the leftovers of this curry into an epic peanut and squash curry soup.
All you have to do is add some vegetable stock to suit your slurping preference!

Melt the coconut oil in a wide-bottomed saucepan set over a medium heat. Add the onion and cook for 2 minutes before adding the squash. Place a lid on the pan and cook for 5 minutes.

While this is cooking, put the coconut milk and peanut butter in a smoothie maker or small blender and blitz until no lumps are visible.

Now back to the saucepan. The squash will have softened but still have a bit of bite, which is perfect. Add the chickpeas, dried fruit, spices and some salt and pepper. Turn up the heat to high and cook for 2 minutes, stirring continuously. Add the water and let it boil for 2 minutes more before removing the pan from the heat. Once the curry stops bubbling, pour in the coconut and peanut mixture and keep stirring until it thickens up slightly.

Ladle into bowls, garnish with the chopped fresh coriander and serve with the rice and a lime wedge on the side.

1 tbsp coconut oil

1 small red onion, peeled and thinly sliced

1 medium-sized butternut squash, peeled and spiralized

1 x 400ml tin of full-fat coconut milk

4 tbsp crunchy peanut butter

1 x 400g tin of chickpeas, drained and rinsed

60g dried fruit, such as raisins, sultanas, goji berries or chopped pitted dates

2½ tbsp good-quality curry powder (check to make sure there's no added sugar)

1 tsp ground turmeric

1 tsp chilli powder (*optional*)

salt and freshly ground black pepper

200ml water

1 tsp chopped fresh coriander, to garnish

cooked brown or wild rice (page 38), to serve

1 lime, cut into wedges, to serve

7.

The good stuff

Nut-free chocolate cups

'Nut-thing' to see here, all you peanut lovers! Seriously, though, these nut-free cups push the peanut butter ones off the charts. They're crunchy, creamy and everything in between.

Line a muffin tin with six silicone or paper cases. If you don't have a muffin tin, just use two cases for added sturdiness.

Break the chocolate into pieces and put in a heatproof bowl set over a saucepan of gently simmering water (a bain-marie), making sure the water doesn't touch the bottom of the bowl. Or you could melt the chocolate in brief bursts in the microwave, stirring regularly.

Divide 100g of the melted chocolate evenly between the cases, spreading the chocolate up the sides to create a cup. Put in the freezer for 5 minutes to harden.

Put the sunflower seed butter, maple syrup and a pinch of salt in a small bowl and mix together. Melt the coconut oil in a small pan set over a medium heat, then add this to the mix. Give everything a good stir to combine fully and make sure the ingredients don't separate. The filling should be smooth and creamy.

Spoon a heaped tablespoon of the filling into each cup. Cover with the remaining melted chocolate and sprinkle over the cacao nibs or buckwheat groats for extra crunch and put back in the freezer for 10 minutes to harden again. You can store these in an airtight container in the fridge for up to two weeks.

175g dark chocolate, at least 80% cocoa solids
3 tbsp sunflower seed butter
3 tbsp maple syrup
pinch of sea salt
2 tbsp coconut oil
2 tbsp cacao nibs or toasted buckwheat groats

Chocolate orange cups

So simple to make, so easy to eat. I didn't share this recipe with anyone for ages because everyone thought it was some fancy recipe that took for ever, and I liked to let them believe that! But nope, no matter how kitchen illiterate you are, you should be able to nail these. If you really love orange, you could add 1 teaspoon of orange zest to the melted chocolate too.

Line a muffin tin with 10 silicone or paper cases. If you don't have a muffin tin, just use two cases for added sturdiness. I used a dome-shaped mould for the cups in the photo to make them look fancy (which gave me six cups, not 10), but a regular muffin tin works just fine.

Break the chocolate into pieces and put in a heatproof bowl set over a saucepan of gently simmering water (a bain-marie), making sure the water doesn't touch the bottom of the bowl. Or you could melt the chocolate in brief bursts in the microwave, stirring regularly. Pour 200g of melted chocolate into a separate bowl so that you're left with 250g of melted chocolate in the first bowl.

Using the bowl with 200g of melted chocolate, use a teaspoon to spread the chocolate up the sides of the cases or moulds to create a cup. Put in the freezer for 5 minutes to harden.

While the chocolate cups are hardening, put the avocado, orange zest and juice (reserve a little zest for decoration at the end), honey, cacao powder and a pinch of salt in a blender and blitz until smooth. Spoon about 1½ teaspoons of this chocolate cream into each case or mould, then cover with the rest of the melted chocolate and sprinkle with an extra pinch of sea salt and a little extra orange zest as decoration.

Put back in the freezer for 10 minutes to harden again. You can store these in an airtight container in the fridge for up to two weeks.

450g good-quality dark chocolate, at least 75% cocoa solids
1 large ripe avocado, peeled, stoned and diced
zest and juice of 1 large orange
3 tbsp honey or maple syrup
1 tbsp raw cacao powder
2 pinches of sea salt

Almond crunch biscuits

These may seem too simple to be true, but they are the ultimate sweet crunch and my favourite biscuit to make, hands down! You can vary this by using peanut butter instead of almond butter.

200g flaked almonds
5 tbsp desiccated coconut
pinch of sea salt
6 tbsp honey or maple syrup
3 tbsp almond or peanut butter
100g dark chocolate (*optional*)

Preheat the oven to 200°C. Scatter the almonds on a baking tray in a single layer and toast in the preheated oven for 8 minutes, stirring now and then, until golden. After the first 3 minutes, add the desiccated coconut to the tray to toast that too. Put the toasted almonds, coconut and a pinch of salt in a medium-sized bowl and stir to combine.

Put the honey and almond butter in a small saucepan set over a medium heat and let them melt together, then stir to combine. Bring to a gentle boil and continue to stir for 2 to 3 minutes. The mix will start to lift up from the bottom of the pan when you stir it and become really thick, like a heavy caramel. Once this happens, pour it over the almonds and work quickly to stir it into the dry ingredients, making sure you cover the nuts completely.

Break the dough into small portions (aim for 1 to 1½ tablespoons per biscuit) and mould each one into a thick cookie shape, but be careful as the dough will be hot. Place the biscuits on a baking tray and put in the freezer to set for 20 minutes.

Meanwhile, if you want to add a drizzle of dark chocolate to the finished biscuits or even dip them in the chocolate, break the chocolate into pieces and put in a heatproof bowl set over a saucepan of gently simmering water (a bain-marie), making sure the water doesn't touch the bottom of the bowl. Or you could melt the chocolate in brief bursts in the microwave, stirring regularly.

Once the biscuits have set, drizzle with or dip in the melted chocolate and put back in the freezer for 5 minutes more to set. You can store these in an airtight container in the fridge for up to two weeks.

BRB
CHOCOLATE
MILK

Notella biscuits

My Notella balls were the biggest hit of my last book. It would have been a shame not to rival them with another epic Notella treat, so here you go – introducing these crunchy, nutty, chocolatey bad boys!

Preheat the oven to 180°C. Line a baking tray with non-stick baking paper.

Start by putting the hazelnuts in a food processor or blender (I use my NutriBullet for this) and pulsing them into a flour – you're aiming for a texture similar to ground almonds, so it doesn't have to be too fine. Tip out into a medium-sized bowl and stir in the cacao powder and baking powder. Using your hands, work in the coconut oil and honey until you have a firm dough.

Taking 1 tablespoon of dough at a time, roll each portion into a ball, then place on the lined tray and press it flat until each biscuit is about 1cm high.

Bake in the preheated oven for 10 minutes. The biscuits will spread a little but they won't be firm, so don't try to lift them from the tray as soon as they come out of the oven. Let the tray sit on a wire rack for 5 to 10 minutes – this is when the cookies will set and develop a delicious crunch.

While the biscuits are baking, break the chocolate into pieces and put in a heatproof bowl set over a saucepan of gently simmering water (a bain-marie), making sure the water doesn't touch the bottom of the bowl. Or you could melt the chocolate in brief bursts in the microwave, stirring regularly.

Once the biscuits have cooled, drizzle them with the melted chocolate and sprinkle with the chopped roasted hazelnuts. These are really killer served with the chocolate milk on page 51. You can store any leftovers in an airtight container for up to a week.

200g skinless hazelnuts

2 tbsp raw cacao powder

1 tsp baking powder or xanthan gum

2 tbsp coconut oil, at room temperature

2 tbsp honey or maple syrup

50g dark chocolate

25g roasted hazelnuts, chopped, to decorate

Digestive biscuits

This one is for all the dads who love their biscuit break – I'm talking about my dad here! It's the simple changes like making your favourite snack or treat from scratch that help make the daily struggle to eat better and feel great easier.

Preheat the oven to 180°C. Line a baking tray with non-stick baking paper.

Put the oat flour and baking soda in a bowl and mix to combine, then add the coconut oil and use your fingertips to rub it into the dry ingredients until the mix is like breadcrumbs. Add the beaten egg and stevia powder and stir to combine into a dough.

Dust a cutting board with a little oat flour, then tip the dough out onto the board and roll it out until it's about 5mm thick. Using a round cookie cutter, a scone cutter or even the rim of a small glass, stamp out 12 biscuits and place them on the lined tray.

Bake in the preheated oven for 15 minutes, then let the tray cool on a wire rack before gently lifting the biscuits off the tray.

If you want to make chocolate digestives, break the chocolate into pieces and put in a heatproof bowl set over a saucepan of gently simmering water (a bain-marie), making sure the water doesn't touch the bottom of the bowl. Or you could melt the chocolate in brief bursts in the microwave, stirring regularly.

Once the biscuits have cooled, spoon a little melted chocolate on the tops, then smooth it out to the edges with a palette knife or the back of the spoon. To get that signature digestive look, use the tines of a fork to make lines down and then across each biscuit. You can store these in an airtight container for up to 10 days.

120g oat flour, plus extra for
    dusting
¾ tsp baking soda
2 tbsp coconut oil, at room
    temperature
1 egg, beaten
2 tbsp stevia powder
50g dark chocolate (*optional*)

Cookie dough

A roll of cookie dough in the fridge was a bit of a luxury item in our house, but I could never stop myself from slicing off a sneaky sliver. I usually ate it raw, but sometimes I managed to bake one or two. I love having a jar of this in the fridge, pre-rolled into balls, ready to eat raw or bake as you want them.

Put the ground almonds, maple syrup, almond butter, coconut flour, coconut oil and vanilla in a medium-sized bowl. Use a spoon to work the ingredients into a dough, then mix in the chocolate chips.

You have two options at this point. You can roll the dough into balls and store them in an airtight container in the fridge to eat raw, but if you feel like having baked cookies, preheat the oven to 180°C and line a baking tray with non-stick baking paper. Press each ball down until it's 5cm thick, place on the tray and bake in the preheated oven for 10 minutes, until golden around the edges. Let them cool and firm up for 5 to 8 minutes before tucking in.

Stored in an airtight container in the fridge, the raw cookie dough will last for up to 12 days or baked cookies for five.

125g ground almonds

4 tbsp maple syrup

2 tbsp smooth almond butter

1½ tbsp coconut flour

1 tbsp coconut oil

1 tsp vanilla paste or powder

2 tbsp dark chocolate chips

Hero cookies

These aren't called hero cookies for nothing! They're the fallback quick treat that everyone wants the recipe for. It's really important to let them set for 5 minutes to firm up after baking, as it creates a nice crunch and it also means the cookies won't burn the tongue off you.

Preheat the oven to 200°C. Line a baking tray with non-stick baking paper.

Put all the ingredients except the chocolate chips in a medium-sized bowl and use the back of a spoon to work together into a dough.

Pinch off portions of the dough and roll into balls – you should get eight cookies – then place on the lined tray and press down until the cookies are about 1.5cm thick. Put two or three chocolate chips on top of each cookie and gently press them into the dough.

Bake in the preheated oven for 6 to 8 minutes, until the cookies are lightly browned around the edges. Put the tray on a wire rack and let the cookies cool for 5 minutes to firm up before carefully sliding them off the tray with a spatula. You can store these in an airtight container for up to three days.

55g whey protein powder or a vegan protein blend, such as rice/hemp

5 tbsp almond butter

3 tbsp honey (you can use maple syrup, but you'll need to use 4 tbsp)

1 tbsp coconut oil, at room temperature

pinch of sea salt

handful of chocolate chips

Protein-packed rocky road

If you manage to make this rocky road without eating some of the squares along the way, you deserve a high five!

You'll need a large ice cube tray or a silicone mini muffin tray to make these.

Grab three small breakfast bowls. Put the ingredients for the three different flavours in separate bowls and use the back of a spoon to combine each one into a dough. Roll each dough into a ball with your hands, then pat it down into a rectangle and cut into 1cm cubes. Put the chunks back in their separate bowls and stash them in the freezer while you melt the chocolate. I should mention that the biscuit base can get a little wet from the coconut oil, which is why you need to keep it in the freezer to set and stay hard.

Break the chocolate into pieces and put in a heatproof bowl set over a saucepan of gently simmering water (a bain-marie), making sure the water doesn't touch the bottom of the bowl, and let it melt. Or you could melt the chocolate in brief bursts in the microwave, stirring regularly.

Once the chocolate has fully melted, carefully open the tin of chilled coconut milk – whatever you do, don't shake the tin after chilling it! – and scoop out the coconut cream at the top of the tin. You should get about 5 tablespoons. Stir this cream into the melted chocolate and save the coconut milk for another use.

Pour 1½ tablespoons of the melted chocolate mix into each mould, then add one or two cubes of each type of dough. Put in the freezer to set for 15 to 20 minutes, then pop the pieces out of the moulds and store in an airtight container in the fridge for up to a week.

250g dark chocolate
1 x 400ml tin of full-fat coconut milk, chilled in the fridge

FOR THE VANILLA CHUNKS:
1 tbsp vanilla whey protein powder
1½ tsp honey
1½ tsp almond or cashew butter

FOR THE STRAWBERRY CHUNKS:
1 tbsp strawberry whey protein powder
1½ tsp honey or maple syrup
1½ tsp almond or cashew butter

FOR THE BISCUIT CHUNKS:
2 tbsp coconut flour
1 tbsp coconut oil
1 tsp honey

Peanut butter brownies

What's better than fudgy, gooey brownies? How about ones with a little peanut butter crunch? You can thank me later.

Preheat the oven to 170°C. Line a 15cm square brownie tin with non-stick baking paper.

Put the peanut butter, cacao powder, maple syrup, vanilla, baking powder and a pinch of salt in a medium-sized bowl. Stir to combine into a smooth batter.

In a separate bowl, use a fork to mash the bananas into a thick purée (don't blend or whisk them). Add the mashed bananas to the peanut butter mixture and combine well, then pour the batter into the lined brownie tin.

Bake in the preheated oven for 25 minutes, until firm on top and lightly crisp along the edges. Let the brownies cool completely on a wire rack while you make the ganache. If the brownies are still warm when you add the ganache, it will melt.

To make the ganache, put the peanut ganache ingredients in a small saucepan set over a low heat and stir until they have melted together. Do the same for the chocolate ganache in a separate saucepan. Drizzle over the brownies and swirl the two ganaches into one another with the handle of a spoon.

Once the ganache has cooled, cut the brownies into squares. You can store any leftovers in an airtight container in the fridge for up to four days.

200g smooth peanut butter

4 tbsp raw cacao powder

4 tbsp maple syrup

1 tsp vanilla extract

½ tsp baking powder

pinch of sea salt

1½ ripe bananas, peeled

FOR THE PEANUT GANACHE:

2 tbsp coconut oil

2 tbsp peanut butter

1 tbsp maple syrup

FOR THE CHOCOLATE GANACHE:

100g dark chocolate, broken into pieces

5 tbsp coconut milk (from a tin, not the drinking kind from a carton)

Raw peanut butter brownie cake

Need a nifty dessert? Here's one that you can prep in advance for parties or dinner guests to impress and destress. It needs to set in the freezer for a few hours, but it takes only minutes to make.

To make the base, break the chocolate into pieces and put in a heatproof bowl set over a saucepan of gently simmering water (a bain-marie), making sure the water doesn't touch the bottom of the bowl, and let it melt. Or you could melt the chocolate in brief bursts in the microwave, stirring regularly.

Put the melted chocolate in a food processor with the almonds and dates and pulse until the mixture is like breadcrumbs. Tip into a 20cm springform tin and press down firmly to create an even layer. Set aside to chill in the fridge while you make the topping.

Melt the coconut oil in a small saucepan set over a low heat. Stir in the peanut butter and maple syrup until they are fully combined with the oil – you don't want these ingredients to separate. Remove from the heat and stir in the peanuts; then pour over the base. Put back in the fridge for 2 to 3 hours, until set.

To serve, release the catch on the springform tin and remove the cake. Melt the chocolate the same way that you did before, then drizzle it all over the top of the cake. Scatter over the peanuts and mint leaves, then cut into slices.

FOR THE BASE:
50g dark chocolate
200g almonds
150g pitted dates

FOR THE TOPPING:
150g coconut oil
200g smooth peanut butter
150g maple syrup or agave
100g roasted peanuts, roughly
    chopped or crushed

TO DECORATE:
60g dark chocolate
handful of roasted peanuts,
    roughly chopped
fresh mint leaves, torn

Diva protein bar

We all know someone who turns into a diva when they're hungry, like Aretha Franklin and Liza Minnelli in those commercials for a certain candy bar a few years back. If you need a treat fast, the diva protein bar will come to your rescue!

Put all the base ingredients in a small breakfast bowl and mix into a dough. Tip out onto a cutting board and roll the dough until it's 2cm thick, then pat into a rectangle.

Using the same bowl, mix the peanut butter, maple syrup and coconut oil together, then spread this evenly over the base. Sprinkle over the peanuts and gently press them down to stick.

Break the chocolate into pieces and put in a heatproof bowl set over a saucepan of gently simmering water (a bain-marie), making sure the water doesn't touch the bottom of the bowl, and let it melt. Or you could melt the chocolate in brief bursts in the microwave, stirring regularly.

Drizzle the melted chocolate over the bar and place in the fridge for 10 minutes to set. Either serve as one large bar or cut in half to make two.

FOR THE BASE:

2 tbsp vanilla whey protein powder (or coconut flour if you don't need the protein)

1½ tbsp smooth peanut butter

1 tbsp honey or maple syrup

FOR THE TOPPING:

2 tsp smooth peanut butter

1 tsp maple syrup

1 tsp coconut oil

handful of roasted peanuts

20g dark chocolate

Fruit crumble skillet

I couldn't leave out a crumble on the good stuff front. It's the dessert I always go for on a menu. My mum makes a mean crumble and she has turned me into a crumble connoisseur!

Preheat the oven to 200°C.

Heat the oil in a large ovenproof frying pan set over a medium-high heat. Add the fruit and cook, stirring, for 6 to 8 minutes, until softened. Stir in the lemon juice, honey and mixed spice and remove from the heat.

While the fruit is cooking, make the topping. Melt the coconut oil in a small saucepan set over a low heat. Put the nuts, oats and sweetener in a medium-sized bowl and stir together, then pour in the melted coconut oil and stir again until well combined. Sprinkle the crumble topping over the fruit in the pan in an even layer.

Transfer the pan to the preheated oven and bake for 10 minutes, until the crumble topping is golden brown and crisp. Serve with a dollop of coconut or Greek yogurt on top.

1 tbsp coconut oil
8 apples, pears or nectarines, peeled, cored and diced
juice of 1 lemon
2 tbsp honey or maple syrup
1 tbsp mixed spice
coconut or Greek yogurt, to serve

FOR THE CRUMBLE:
2 tbsp coconut oil
130g walnuts, pecans or your favourite nut, roughly chopped
120g porridge oats
2 tbsp honey, maple syrup or coconut sugar

Dark chocolate soufflé

Another blast from the past! My sister and I used to make chocolate soufflés all the time as kids, as it was our favourite quick dessert. We weren't sophisticated enough to use dark chocolate back then, but I'm sure the kids nowadays are miles ahead of us on the trends.

Preheat the oven to 190°C. Place two ramekins on a baking tray to make it easier to put them into the oven.

Whisk the egg whites in a spotlessly clean, dry bowl until stiff.

Break the chocolate into pieces and put in a heatproof bowl set over a saucepan of gently simmering water (a bain-marie), making sure the water doesn't touch the bottom of the bowl. Stir in the egg yolks and honey until well combined.

Fold the melted chocolate into the fluffy egg whites, trying not to knock out any air. Spoon this mix into the ramekins and bake in the preheated oven for 10 to 15 minutes, depending on how gooey you like your soufflé. Serve immediately before the soufflés fall!

4 eggs, separated
150g dark chocolate, at least 70% cocoa solids
2 tbsp honey or maple syrup

Protein soufflés, two ways

You may have spotted a trend here by now: my love of gooey sweet treats! When I came up with this recipe it was like *Ready Steady Cook* – I had only a few ingredients at hand – but now it's a regular go-to recipe that I can make in minutes.

Preheat the oven to 180°C. Place two ramekins on a baking tray to make it easier to put them into the oven.

If you're making the sweet potato soufflé, start by steaming the sweet potato for 12 to 15 minutes, until completely tender. Pat dry to remove any excess water.

Put the steamed sweet potato or the banana in a food processor or blender (a NutriBullet works well) along with the eggs and blitz until smooth. Add the nut butter and protein powder and blend again for 30 seconds.

Pour the batter into the ramekins and bake for 8 to 10 minutes, until the soufflés have risen and are golden on top but still a little gooey on the inside. Serve immediately before the soufflés fall!

FOR THE SWEET POTATO SOUFFLÉ:

1 small sweet potato, peeled and cut into chunks

2 eggs

2 tbsp almond butter

1 scoop of chocolate whey protein powder

FOR THE BANANA SOUFFLÉ:

1 large ripe banana, peeled

2 eggs

2 tbsp cashew butter

2 scoops of vanilla whey protein powder

Banana donuts

Mmmm, donuts! Let your inner Homer Simpson out for these. This is a simple recipe for any donut lovers looking to replace their typical splurge.

Preheat the oven to 190°C.

Start by making the topping. Put the coconut oil, honey, cashew butter and cinnamon in a small saucepan and melt together over a medium-high heat to create a thick, creamy caramel. Simmer for 2 minutes, stirring constantly, until the edges begin to bubble, then pour into a bowl and place in the fridge until you're ready to coat the donuts. The mix will harden in the fridge, becoming an awesome ganache-style frosting.

Put the banana, egg, ground almonds, honey, peanut butter, cinnamon and ginger in a blender and blitz into a smooth batter, then stir in the walnuts. Using a non-stick six-cavity donut pan, divide the batter between four of the moulds. (If you don't have a special donut pan, don't despair – check out my tip in the intro to the apple cinnamon donut recipe on page 237.)

Bake in the preheated oven for about 12 minutes, until the donuts have risen and are golden brown and firm. Let the donuts cool in the tin for a few minutes before turning them out onto a wire rack to cool completely before you glaze them. Don't be tempted to glaze the donuts while they're still warm or the topping will melt right off.

To finish, spread some of the topping on each cooled donut, then scatter over the crushed pistachios. These are best eaten warm on the day that they're made, but believe it or not, they still taste pretty damn good up to four days later.

1 small ripe banana, peeled

1 egg

5 tbsp ground almonds

2 tbsp honey

1 tbsp smooth peanut butter

1 tsp ground cinnamon

½ tsp ground ginger

2 tbsp chopped walnuts

FOR THE TOPPINGS:

2 tbsp coconut oil

2 tbsp honey or maple syrup

1 tbsp cashew butter

1 tsp ground cinnamon or ground cardamom (I love cardamom here!)

2 tbsp crushed pistachios or your favourite nut

Apple cinnamon donuts

These are a cinch to make if you have a non-stick donut pan, which you can get online or in a good kitchen supply shop, but I have an easy trick for making them even if you don't have a special pan. Just cut a sheet of foil into 4 x 15cm squares. Grabbing the centre of each square of foil, create a cone shape. Press each square into the muffin tin and spray well with cooking oil to grease it. Job done!

Preheat the oven to 190°C.

Start by making the topping. Put the coconut oil, honey, almond butter and cinnamon in a small saucepan set over a medium-high heat and melt together to create a thick, creamy caramel. Simmer for 2 minutes, stirring constantly, until the edges begin to bubble. Pour into a bowl and place in the fridge until you're ready to coat the donuts. The mix will harden in the fridge, becoming an awesome ganache-style frosting.

Put one-quarter of the grated apple and all the other ingredients in a blender and blitz until smooth. There will still be some small bits of apple, but that's okay. Stir in the rest of the grated apple, then divide the batter between four donut moulds.

Bake in the preheated oven for about 12 minutes, until the donuts have risen and are golden brown and firm. Let the donuts cool in the tin for a few minutes before turning them out onto a wire rack to cool completely before you glaze them. Don't be tempted to glaze the donuts while they're still warm or the topping will melt right off.

To finish, spread some of the topping on each cooled donut, then scatter over the flaked almonds. These are best eaten warm on the day that they're made, but believe it or not, they still taste pretty damn good up to four days later.

¾ small apple, grated

1 egg

6 tbsp ground almonds

2 tbsp honey

1 tbsp almond butter

1 tsp ground cinnamon

1 tsp vanilla powder

½ tsp ground nutmeg

FOR THE TOPPINGS:

2 tbsp coconut oil

2 tbsp honey or maple syrup

1 tbsp smooth almond or peanut butter

1 tsp ground cinnamon

2 tbsp toasted flaked almonds

Berry crumble parfait

Light and refreshing, this is the perfect BBQ or summertime dessert. Plus if you prep it in advance, it's a no-brainer – just keep each component in a separate airtight container and assemble it just before serving.

Preheat the oven to 200°C.

Put the berries, ginger, orange juice and maple syrup in a small saucepan set over a medium heat. Simmer for 5 to 6 minutes, until the berries have broken down. Remove from the heat and leave to cool.

Meanwhile, to make the crumble, combine all the ingredients in a bowl, then spread out evenly on a baking tray. Bake in the preheated oven for 15 minutes, until toasted, then set aside to cool.

To layer up the parfait in jars or sundae glasses, start with 2 tablespoons of the stewed berries, then add 2 tablespoons of the crumble and top with 2 tablespoons of Greek yogurt. Repeat the layers all the way up to the top of the jar or glass.

500g Greek yogurt

FOR THE STEWED BERRIES:
500g fresh berries, such as
    raspberries, blueberries and
    blackberries
5cm piece of fresh ginger,
    peeled and grated
juice of 1 orange
4 tbsp maple syrup

FOR THE CRUMBLE:
150g flaked almonds
100g ground almonds
100g ground hazelnuts
2 tbsp coconut oil or butter
1 tbsp maple syrup

Easy oat sponge

I'm not trying to get all fancy on you, but check out this Victoria sponge with that gorgeous filling!

Preheat the oven to 180°C. Line 2 x 20cm sandwich tins with non-stick baking paper, then lightly grease the paper with coconut oil or butter, otherwise the oat flour base tends to stick to the paper.

Put the oats in a blender and whizz to a fine flour consistency.

Put the eggs in a large bowl and whisk with a balloon whisk for 3 to 4 minutes, until they turn pale yellow and frothy. Slowly tip in the stevia, vinegar and baking powder. While still whisking the eggs, add the oat flour a little at a time until it has all been incorporated.

Pour half the batter into each prepared tin and bake in the preheated oven for 15 minutes, until golden and a skewer inserted into the centre comes out clean. Let the cakes cool in the tin for 5 minutes before turning out onto a wire rack to cool completely. If you add the yogurt filling while the cakes are still warm, it will melt off.

To make the filling, combine the Greek yogurt and protein powder or casein (if using) into a smooth, thick cream. The protein powder or casein will thicken the yogurt to give it a nice buttercream consistency, but it's not necessary to add it.

If you're not going to eat the cake straight away, wait to add the filling until you're ready to serve. Place one cake on a large platter or cake stand. Spoon the yogurt into the middle of the cake, add most of the fresh berries and nestle the other sponge on top, pressing down gently to spread out the filling. Top with the rest of the berries and sprinkle with some stevia powder or drizzle with a little honey (if using).

coconut oil or butter, for greasing
150g porridge oats
6 eggs
4 tbsp stevia powder, plus extra to decorate
1 tbsp apple cider vinegar
1 tsp baking powder
honey, for drizzling (optional)

FOR THE FILLING:
250g Greek yogurt or your favourite yogurt
1 scoop of vanilla whey protein powder or vanilla casein (optional)
150g fresh berries, chopped if large

Mint chocolate chip sundae

Have you ever tried gelato? It's ice cream's good-looking cousin, and this, my friends, is pretty damn close, texture-wise. Plus the taste is the perfect balance between sweet and refreshing.

Put the frozen bananas, cacao nibs, mint leaves, honey and cacao powder in a blender or food processor and blitz until smooth. Scoop into a sundae glass, drizzle with the chocolate sauce and top with a hero cookie. Serve immediately before it starts to melt.

4 bananas, peeled, sliced
    and frozen
handful of cacao nibs
4 fresh mint leaves
4 tbsp honey or maple syrup
2 tbsp raw cacao powder
chocolate sauce (page 35), to
    serve
2 hero cookies (page 217)

HERO COOKIE

Berry quick sorbet

These three simple ingredients make a delicious sin-free sorbet in minutes. This recipe proves that a whole foods approach doesn't rule out any of your favourite things – it just changes them a little.

This couldn't be easier: just blend everything together for 40 to 60 seconds, until smooth, then pour into a small airtight container and freeze for 20 minutes to set.

400g frozen berries

4 tbsp maple syrup

juice of 1 lime

INDEX

I OWE YOU ONE ...

I will start with my sister, Rachel, who puts up with the most. She spends all her free time helping me with Natural Born Feeder, brainstorming and putting my sometimes crazy and unrealistic ideas into fruition. She also does the majority of the cleaning-up after I've finished making a mess in the kitchen!

To my family who helped me with my pop-up café last year. I think we can all agree we won't forget that one – particularly my dad – and none of us will ever roll as many Notella balls in one sitting again! Thank you for your continued support and encouragement, and for ultimately sparking my passion for cooking.

Shout out to my friends, who are the most fabulous bunch of guinea pigs, who never complain and are brutally honest when needed!

To my editor, Kristin Jensen, I can't believe you said yes to another book! I love when I get an email from you because I know it's the beginning of something creative. I couldn't imagine working with anyone else. I have learned so much from you and you have changed my style of writing and helped with how I approached this book. Somehow you manage to make editing one of the most enjoyable parts of creating a cookbook, and, as any author knows, that's often far from the truth!

To my shoot team, Jo Murphy, Orla Neligan, Jane Flanagan, Sarah Watchorn and Barry Hirst, thank you for your patience and incredible work and for still talking to me! We all worked long, tiring days and I truly appreciate that you gave me and this book so much time, thought and sweat!

To Jonathan Conway, my literary agent, thank you so much for going above and beyond. Every step of the way you have always been so involved and your belief in me and Natural Born Feeder is both motivating and heart-warming.

To Claire Pelly, Michael McLoughlin and all the team at Penguin Random House Ireland, what can I say?! Thank you for being so welcoming and making me even more excited about this book than anything else before. Your enthusiasm about *Half Hour Hero* is the reason you have been incredible to work with. Also, thank you for taking a chance with me, giving me such control and pulling all the elements together to create exactly what I hoped *Half Hour Hero* would be.

Lastly, this is the big one . . . to all of you – the readers, the Natural Born Feeder community online and offline, everyone who called into my pop-up café or recreated recipes – you are the inspiration for this book and through speaking with you, engaging on social media, reading your comments and listening to you, grew the idea of *Half Hour Hero* – this book is as much yours as it is mine!

PENGUIN IRELAND

UK | USA | Canada | Ireland | Australia
India | New Zealand | South Africa

Penguin Ireland is part of the Penguin Random House group of companies
whose addresses can be found at global.penguinrandomhouse.com.

First published 2017

001

Copyright © Rozanna Purcell, 2017
Photography copyright © Joanne Murphy, 2017

Printed in Germany by Mohn Media
Colour reproduction by Altaimage Ltd

A CIP catalogue record for this book is available from the British Library

ISBN: 978–1–844–88418–6

FSC
www.fsc.org

MIX
Paper from
responsible sources
FSC® C018179